DeFi
AND THE
FUTURE
OF
FINANCE

DeFi
AND THE
FUTURE
OF
FINANCE

Campbell R. Harvey
Ashwin Ramachandran
Joey Santoro

WILEY

Published by John Wiley & Sons, Inc., Hoboken, New Jersey.

Published simultaneously in Canada.

For general information on our other products and services or for technical support, please contact our Customer Care Department within the United States at (800) 762-2974, outside the United States at (317) 572-3993 or fax (317) 572-4002.

Wiley publishes in a variety of print and electronic formats and by print-on-demand. Some material included with standard print versions of this book may not be included in e-books or in print-on-demand. If this book refers to media such as a CD or DVD that is not included in the version you purchased, you may download this material at http://booksupport.wiley.com. For more information about Wiley products, visit www.wiley.com.

Library of Congress Cataloging-in-Publication Data is Available:

ISBN 9781119836018 (Hardcover)
ISBN 9781119836032 (ePDF)
ISBN 9781119836025 (ePub)

COVER DESIGN: PAUL MCCARTHY
COVER IMAGES: GETTY IMAGES: © TUOMAS LEHTINEN

SKY10031223_110421

CONTENTS

Contents

FOREWORD

D_{eFi} is a cute acronym for "decentralized finance," but it obfuscates its true potential: a new financial system built from the ground up. While DeFi is small today—containing, as of this writing, tens of billions of dollars in assets relative to the hundreds of trillions in the traditional financial system—it is growing rapidly. And while its rise will take decades, I believe DeFi will be the primary financial system of the world.

Why? DeFi is a true "internet of money." The internet showed the power of a universal, open network for information. In 40 years the idea of a similarly open, global network for value transfer will seem obvious, which makes this a truth hiding in plain sight today.

As with any new technology, crypto and the new decentralized financial system built atop it will be different from its old-world analogue. DeFi is unique relative to the traditional financial system because it is permissionless, open access, global, composable, and transparent. No longer are centralized institutions needed for basic financial actions. In DeFi, you can be your own bank and get credit from code on a blockchain—no institution required!

Yet so little of the infrastructure of this ecosystem has been built. We are perhaps 1 percent, likely less, into DeFi as a phenomenon. A burgeoning ecosystem of developers around the world is currently constructing the financial building blocks of tomorrow. At our crypto investment firm Paradigm, we often ask ourselves, "If there were a periodic table of financial primitives, what has been built today and what is left to fill in?" That is the opportunity for entrepreneurs.

DeFi, like the internet, will likely make financial services cheaper, faster, secure, personalized, and more. If YouTube grew the breadth of video content by orders of magnitude because it was free and easy for anyone to both create and use videos, what will DeFi do for financial products as it similarly allows anyone to create and use anything at near-zero cost?

That future has yet to be written. This book provides a peek into that future, and you, the reader, hold the power to create it.

Fred Ehrsam
Co-founder and Managing Partner, Paradigm
Co-founder, Coinbase

PREFACE

Decentralized finance (or DeFi) has always been a big part of what I hoped to see people build on Ethereum. Ideas around user-issued assets, stablecoins, prediction markets, decentralized exchanges, and much more had already been at the top of my mind as well as the minds of many others trying to build the next stage of blockchain technology in those special early days of 2013–14. But instead of creating a limited platform targeting a set of known existing use cases, as many others did, Ethereum introduced general-purpose programmability, allowing blockchain-based contracts that can hold digital assets and transfer them according to pre-defined rules, and even support applications with components that are not financial at all.

People in the Ethereum community started working on applications such as on-chain stablecoins, prediction markets, and exchanges almost immediately, but only after more than five years did the ecosystem truly start to mature. I believe that DeFi will create a new, easy-to-use and globally accessible financial system for the world. For example, applications like stablecoins are some of the most valuable innovations to come out of DeFi so far. They allow anyone in the world to benefit from the censorship resistance, self-sovereignty, and instant global accessibility of cryptocurrency while having the purchasing power stability of the dollar—or, if the dollar ever stops being stable, they enable people to quickly move their funds into another asset that does a better job of maintaining stability.

So why is DeFi important? Financial censorship continues to be a problem for marginalized groups, with restrictions and imposed hardships often going far beyond what is actually required by any law. This is doubly true once we start looking beyond the relatively safe bubble of developed countries. DeFi greatly reduces the cost of experimentation, making it much easier to build a new application, and smart contracts with verifiable open-source code greatly reduce the barrier of needing to trust the founding team to manage funds. DeFi offers "composability," allowing new applications to easily and immediately interoperate with any other applications that already exist. These are serious improvements over the traditional financial system, and ones that I believe remain under-appreciated.

In the book *DeFi and The Future of Finance*, the authors discuss many of the additional improvements DeFi offers over the traditional financial system. The authors also explain the in-depth workings of many of the most important DeFi protocols today, including stablecoins, automated market makers, and more. I recommend this book to anyone interested in learning more about Ethereum and DeFi protocols.

Vitalik Buterin
Co-founder of Ethereum

I

INTRODUCTION

We have come full circle. The earliest form of market exchange was peer to peer, also known as barter.[1] Barter was highly inefficient because supply and demand had to be exactly matched between peers. To solve the matching problem, money was introduced as a medium of exchange and store of value. Initial types of money were not centralized. Agents accepted any number of items such as stones or shells in exchange for goods. Eventually, specie money emerged, a form in which the currency had tangible value. Today, we have non-collateralized (fiat) currency controlled by central banks. The form of money has changed over time, but the basic infrastructure of financial institutions has not.

However, the scaffolding is emerging for a historic disruption of our current financial infrastructure. DeFi, or decentralized finance, seeks to build and combine open-source financial building blocks into sophisticated products with minimized friction and maximized value to users utilizing blockchain technology. Given it costs no more to provide services to a customer with $100 or $100 million in assets, we believe that DeFi will replace all meaningful centralized financial infrastructure in the future. This is a technology of inclusion whereby anyone can pay the flat fee to use and benefit from the innovations of DeFi.

DeFi is fundamentally a competitive marketplace of decentralized financial applications that function as various financial "primitives" such as exchange, save, lend, and tokenize. These applications benefit from the network effects of combining and recombining DeFi products and attracting increasingly more market share from the traditional financial ecosystem.

Our book details the problems that DeFi solves: **centralized control, limited access, inefficiency, lack of interoperability,** and **opacity**. We then describe the current and rapidly growing DeFi landscape and present a vision of the future opportunities that DeFi unlocks. Let's begin with the problems.

FIVE KEY PROBLEMS OF CENTRALIZED FINANCIAL SYSTEMS

For centuries, we have lived in a world of centralized finance. Central banks control the money supply. Financial trading is largely done via intermediaries. Borrowing and lending are conducted through traditional banking institutions. In the last few years, however, considerable progress has been made on a much different model: decentralized finance. In this framework, peers interact with peers via a common ledger not controlled by any centralized organization. DeFi offers considerable potential for solving the following five key problems associated with centralized finance: centralized control, limited access, inefficiency, lack of inoperability, and opacity.

1. ***Centralized Control.*** Centralization has many layers. Most consumers and businesses deal with a single, localized bank, which controls rates and fees. Switching is possible, but it can be costly. Further, the U.S. banking system is highly concentrated. The four largest banks have a 44 percent share of insured deposits compared with 15 percent in 1984.[2] Interestingly, the U.S. banking system is less concentrated than other countries, such as the United Kingdom and Canada. In a centralized banking system, one consolidated entity attempts to set short-term interest rates and to influence the rate of inflation.

   This phenomenon reaches beyond the legacy financial sector to tech players like Amazon, Facebook, and Google, who now dominate industries like retail sales and digital advertising.

2. ***Limited Access.*** Today, 1.7 billion people are unbanked, making it very challenging for them to

obtain loans and to operate in the world of internet commerce. Further, many consumers must resort to payday lending operations to cover liquidity shortfalls. Being banked, however, does not guarantee access. For example, a bank may not want to bother with the small loan that a new business requires. Instead, it may suggest a credit card loan, which carries with it a borrowing rate well above 20 percent per year – a high hurdle rate for finding profitable investment projects.

3. **Inefficiency**. A centralized financial system has many inefficiencies. Perhaps the most egregious example is the credit card interchange rate that causes consumers and small businesses to lose up to 3 percent of a transaction's value with every swipe due to the payment network oligopoly's pricing power. Remittance fees are 5–7 percent. Time is also wasted in the two days it takes to "settle" a stock transaction (officially transfer ownership). In the Internet age, this seems utterly implausible. Other inefficiencies include costly (and slow) transfer of funds, direct and indirect brokerage fees, lack of security, and the inability to conduct microtransactions, many of which are not obvious to users. In the current banking system, deposit interest rates remain very low and loan rates high because banks need to cover their brick-and-mortar costs. The insurance industry provides another example.

4. ***Lack of Interoperability***. Consumers and businesses deal with financial institutions in an environment that locks interconnectivity. It is well-known that the U.S. financial system is siloed and designed to sustain high switching costs. Moving money from one institution to another can be unduly lengthy and complicated. For example, a wire transfer can take three days to complete.

   In an attempt to mitigate this issue within the world of centralized finance, in 2019 Visa tried to acquire Plaid,[3] a product that allows any company to plug into an institution's information stack with the user's permission. Though this was a strategic move to help Visa buy some time, it did not address the fundamental problems with the current financial infrastructure.

5. ***Opacity***. The current financial system is not transparent. Bank customers have very little information on the financial health of their bank and instead must place their faith in the limited government protection of FDIC insurance on their deposits. Further, it is difficult for them to know if the rate they are offered on a loan is competitive. Although the consumer insurance industry has made some progress with fintech services that offer to find the "lowest" price, the loan market is very fragmented — yet competing lenders all suffer from the system's inefficiencies. The result is that the lowest price still reflects legacy brick-and-mortar and bloated back-office costs.

IMPLICATIONS

The implications of these five problems are twofold. First, many of these costs lead to *lower economic growth*. For example, if loan rates are high because of legacy costs, high-quality investment projects may be foregone, as explained previously. An entrepreneur's high-quality idea may target a 20 percent rate of return – precisely the type of project that accelerates economic growth. If the bank tells the entrepreneur to borrow money on their credit card at 24 percent per year, this seemingly profitable project may never be pursued.

Second, these problems perpetuate or exacerbate *inequality*. Across the political spectrum, most people agree there should be equality of opportunity: a project should be financed based on the quality of the idea and the soundness of the execution plan and not by other factors. Importantly, inequality also limits growth when good ideas are not financed. Though purported to be the land of opportunity, the United States has one of the worst records in migrating income from the bottom quartile to the top quartile.[4] Inequality of opportunity arises, in part, from lack of access to the current banking system, reliance on costly alternative financing such as payday lending, and the inability to buy or sell in the modern world of e-commerce.

These implications are far-reaching, and, by any calculations, this is a long list of serious problems endemic to our current system of centralized finance. Our financial infrastructure has failed to fully adapt to the digital era in which we are living. Decentralized finance offers new opportunities. The technology is nascent, but the upside is potentially transformational.

Our book has multiple goals. First, we identify the weaknesses in the current system, including discussion of some early initiatives that challenged the business models of centralized finance. Next, we explore the origins of decentralized finance. We then discuss a critical component of DeFi: blockchain technology. Next, we detail the solutions DeFi offers and couple this with a deep dive on some leading ideas in this emerging space. We then analyze the major risk factors and conclude by looking to the future and attempt to identify the winners and losers.

II

THE ORIGINS OF MODERN DECENTRALIZED FINANCE

A BRIEF HISTORY OF FINANCE

Even as today's financial system is plagued with inefficiencies, it is far better than those of the past, where market exchanges were peer to peer and bartering required two parties' needs to match exactly. Out of this, an informal credit system emerged in villages whereby people kept a mental record of "gifts."[1]

Modern coinage came much later, first emerging in Lydia around 600 BCE and providing what we think of as today's functions of money: unit of account, medium of exchange, and store of value. Important characteristics of money included durability, portability, divisibility, uniformity, limited supply, acceptability, and stability. Bank notes, originating in China, made their way to Europe in the thirteenth century.

Nonphysical transfer of money originated in 1871 with Western Union. Figure 2.1 shows a copy of an early transfer for $300. Notice how the fees amount to $9.34, or roughly 3 percent. It is remarkable that so little has changed in 150 years: money transfers are routinely more expensive, and credit card fees are 3 percent.

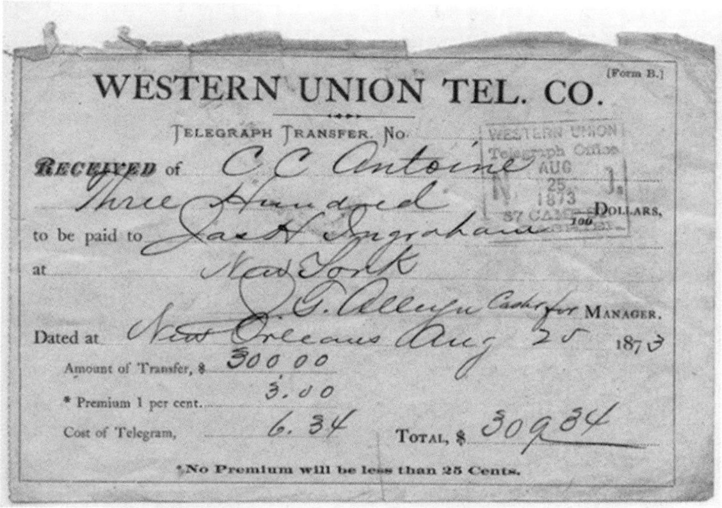

WESTERN UNION TEL. CO. [Form B.]

Telegraph Transfer. No.

WESTERN UNION Telegraph Office AUG 25 1873

Received of C C Antoine

Three Hundred Dollars,

to be paid to Jas H Ingraham

at New York

J. G. Allen Cashr for Manager.

Dated at New Orleans Aug 25 1873

Amount of Transfer, $ 300 00

* Premium 1 per cent. 3.00

Cost of Telegram, 6.34 Total, $ 309 34

*No Premium will be less than 25 Cents.

Figure 2.1 Western Union transfer from 1873
Source: Western Union Holdings, Inc.

The last 75 years has seen many firsts in the financial world: credit card in 1950 (Diners Club); automated teller machine (ATM) in 1967 (Barclays Bank); telephone banking in 1983 (Bank of Scotland); Internet banking in 1994 (Stanford Federal Credit Union); radio-frequency identification (RFID) payments in 1997 (Mobil Speedpass); chip-and-pin credit cards in 2005 (Mastercard); and Apple Pay with a mobile device in 2014 (Apple).

Importantly, all these innovations were built on the backbone of centralized finance. While there have been some technological advances, the structure of today's banking system has not changed much in the past 150 years. That is, digitization still supported a legacy structure. The high costs associated with this legacy system has spurred further advances known as *fintech*.

FINTECH

When costs are high, innovation will arise to capitalize on inefficiencies. Sometimes, however, a powerful layer of middle people can slow this process. An early example of decentralized finance emerged in the foreign currency (forex) market 20 years ago. At the time, large corporations used their investment banks to manage their forex needs. For example, a U.S.-based corporation might need €50 million at the end of September to make a payment on some goods purchased in Germany. Its bank would quote a rate for the transaction. At the same time, another client of the bank might need to sell €50 million at the end of September.

The bank would quote a different rate. The difference in the rate is known as the spread – the profit the bank makes for being the intermediary. Given the multitrillion-dollar forex market, this was an important part of bank profits.

In early 2001, a fintech startup offered the following idea.[2] Instead of individual corporations querying various banks to get the best rate, why not have an electronic system match the buyers and sellers directly at an agreed upon price and *no* spread? Indeed, the bank could offer this service to its own customers and collect a modest fee (compared with the spread). Furthermore, given that some customers deal with multiple banks, it would be possible to connect customers at all banks participating in the peer-to-peer network.

You can imagine the reception. The bank might say: "Are you telling me we should invest in an electronic system that will cannibalize our business and largely eliminate a very important profit center?" However, even 20 years ago, banks realized that their largest customers were very unhappy with the current system. As globalization surged, these customers faced unnecessary forex transactions costs.

An even earlier example was the rise of dark pool stock trading. In 1979, the U.S. Securities and Exchange Commission (SEC) instituted Rule 19c3, which allowed stocks listed on one exchange, such as the New York Stock Exchange (NYSE), to be traded off-exchange. Many large institutions moved their trading large blocks to these dark pools, where they traded peer to peer with far lower costs than traditional exchange-based trading.

The excessive costs of transacting has ushered in many fintech innovations. PayPal,[3] founded more than 20 years ago, is a forerunner in the payments space; in 2017, seven of the largest U.S. banks added their own payment system called Zelle.[4] An important commonality of these cost-reducing fintech advances is that they rely on the centralized backbone of the current financial infrastructure.

BITCOIN AND CRYPTOCURRENCY

The dozens of digital currency initiatives beginning in the early 1980s all failed.[5] The landscape shifted, however, with the publication of the famous Satoshi Nakamoto Bitcoin white paper[6] in 2008, which presents a peer-to-peer system that is decentralized and uses the concept of *blockchain*. Invented in 1991 by Haber and Stornetta,[7] blockchain was initially primarily envisioned to be a time-stamping system to keep track of different versions of a document. The key innovation of Bitcoin was to combine the idea of blockchain (time stamping) with a consensus mechanism called *proof of work* (introduced by Back[8] in 2002). The technology produced an immutable ledger that eliminated a key problem with any digital asset: you can make perfect copies and spend them multiple times. Blockchains allow for the important features desirable in a store of value, which were never before simultaneously present in a single asset. Blockchains allow for cryptographic scarcity (Bitcoin has a fixed supply cap of 21 million), censorship resistance and user sovereignty (no entity other than the user can determine how to use funds), and portability (can send any quantity anywhere for a low flat fee). These features combined in a single technology make cryptocurrency a powerful innovation.

The value proposition of Bitcoin is important and can be best understood juxtaposed with that of other financial assets. For example, consider the U.S. dollar (USD). It used to be backed by gold before the gold standard was abandoned in 1971. Now, the demand for USD comes from (a) taxes, (b) purchase of U.S. goods denominated in USD, and (c) repayment of debt denominated by USD. These three cases create value that is not intrinsic but rather is based on the network that is the U.S. economy. Expansion or contraction in these components can impact the price of the USD. Additionally, shocks to the supply of USD adjust its price at a given level of demand. The Fed can adjust the supply of USD through monetary policy in an attempt to achieve financial or political goals. Inflation eats away at the value of USD, decreasing its ability to store value over time. One might be concerned with runaway inflation – what Paul Tudor Jones calls *the great monetary inflation* – which would lead to a flight to inflation-resistant assets.[9] Gold has proven to be a successful inflation hedge due to its practically limited supply, concrete utility, and general global trustworthiness. However, given that gold is a volatile asset, its historical hedging ability is realized only at extremely long horizons.[10]

Many argue that Bitcoin has no "tangible" value and therefore should be worthless. Continuing the gold comparison, approximately two-thirds of gold is used for jewelry, and an additional amount is used in technology hardware. Gold has tangible value. The U.S. dollar, while a fiat currency, has value as "legal tender." However, there are many examples from history whereby currency emerged without any backing that had value.

A relatively recent example is the Iraqi Swiss dinar. This was the currency of Iraq until the first Gulf War in 1990. The printing plates were manufactured in Switzerland (hence the name), and the printing was outsourced to the United Kingdom. In 1991, Iraq was divided, with the Kurds controlling the north and Saddam Hussein the south. Due to sanctions, Iraq could not import dinars from the UK and had to start local production. In May 1993, the Central Bank of Iraq announced that citizens had three weeks to exchange old 25 dinars for new ones (Figure 2.2). Afterwards, the old dinar would be unredeemable.

The old Iraqi Swiss dinar, however, continued to be used in the north. In the south, the new dinar suffered from extreme inflation. Eventually, the exchange rate was 300 new dinars for a single Iraqi Swiss dinar. The key insight here is that

Figure 2.2   Iraqi Swiss dinars and new dinars
Source: Central Bank of Iraq

the Iraqi Swiss dinar had no official backing – but it was accepted as money. There was no tangible value, yet it had value. Importantly, value can be derived from both tangible and intangible sources.

The features of Bitcoin that we have mentioned – particularly scarcity and self-sovereignty – make it a potential store of value and possible hedge to political and economic unrest at the hands of global governments. As the network grows, the value proposition only increases due to increased trust and liquidity. Although Bitcoin was originally intended as a peer-to-peer currency, its deflationary characteristics and flat fees discourage its use in small transactions. We argue that Bitcoin is the flagship of a new asset class, namely, cryptocurrencies, which can have varied use cases based on the construction of their networks. Bitcoin itself, we believe, will continue to grow as an important store of value and a potential inflation hedge over long horizons.[11]

The original cryptocurrencies offered an alternative to a financial system that had been dominated by governments and centralized institutions such as central banks. They arose largely from a desire to replace inefficient, siloed financial systems with immutable, borderless, open-source algorithms. These new currencies can adjust their parameters such as inflation and mechanism for consensus via their underlying blockchain to create different value propositions. We will discuss blockchain and cryptocurrency in greater depth later on but for now will focus on a particular cryptocurrency with special relevance to DeFi.

ETHEREUM AND DeFi

Ethereum (ETH) is currently the second largest cryptocurrency by market cap ($260b). Vitalik Buterin introduced the idea in 2014, and Ethereum mined its first block in 2015. Ethereum is in some sense a logical extension of the applications of Bitcoin because it allows for *smart contracts* – which are code that lives on a blockchain, can control assets and data, and define interactions between the assets, data, and network participants. The capacity for smart contracts defines Ethereum as a *smart contract platform.*

Ethereum and other smart contract platforms specifically gave rise to the *decentralized application,* or *dApp.* The backend components of these applications are built with interoperable, transparent smart contracts that continue to exist if the chain they live on exists. dApps allow peers to interact directly and remove the need for a company to act as a central clearing house for app interactions. It quickly became apparent that the first killer dApps would be financial ones.

The drive toward financial dApps became the DeFi movement, which seeks to build and combine open-source financial building blocks into sophisticated products with minimized friction and maximized value to users. Because it costs no more at an organization level to provide services to a customer with $100 or $100 million in assets, DeFi proponents believe that all meaningful financial infrastructure will be replaced by smart contracts, which can provide more value to a larger group of users. Anyone can simply pay the flat fee to use the contract and benefit from the innovations of DeFi. We will discuss smart contract platforms and dApps in more depth in Chapter 3.

DeFi is fundamentally a competitive marketplace of financial dApps that function as various financial "primitives" such as exchange, lend, and tokenize. They benefit from the network effects of combining and recombining DeFi products and attracting increasingly more market share from the traditional financial ecosystem. Our goal in this book is to give an overview of the problems that DeFi solves, describe the current and rapidly growing DeFi landscape, and present a vision of the future opportunities that DeFi unlocks.

III

DeFi INFRASTRUCTURE

In this chapter, we discuss the innovations that led to DeFi and lay out the terminology.

BLOCKCHAIN

The key to all DeFi is the decentralizing backbone: a block-chain. Fundamentally, blockchains are software protocols that allow multiple parties to operate under shared assumptions and data without trusting each other. These data can be anything, such as location and destination information of items in a supply chain or account balances of a token. Updates are packaged into "blocks" and are "chained" together cryptographically to allow an audit of the prior history – hence the name.

Blockchains are possible because of *consensus protocols* – sets of rules that determine what kinds of blocks can become part of the chain and thus the "truth." These consensus protocols are designed to resist malicious tampering up to a certain security bound. The blockchains we focus on currently use the *proof of work (PoW)* consensus protocol, which relies on a computationally and energy intensive lottery to determine which block to add. The participants agree that the longest chain of blocks is the truth. If attackers want to make a longer chain that contains malicious transactions, they must outpace all the computational work of the entire rest of the network. In theory, they would need most of the network power ("hash rate") to accomplish this – hence, the famous 51 percent attack being the boundary of PoW security. Luckily, it is extraordinarily difficult for any actor, even an entire country, to amass this much network power on the most widely used blockchains, such as Bitcoin or Ethereum. Even if most of the network power can be temporarily acquired, the amount of block history that can be overwritten is constrained by how long this majority can be maintained.

As long as no malicious party can acquire majority control of the network computational power, the transactions will be processed by the good faith actors and appended to the ledger when a block is "won."

The focus here is on proof of work, but many alternative consensus mechanisms exist, the most important of which is *proof of stake (PoS)*. Validators in PoS commit some capital (the stake) to attest that the block is valid and make themselves available by staking their cryptocurrency. Then, they may be selected to propose a block, which needs to be attested by many of the other validators. Validators profit by both proposing a block and attesting to the validity of others' proposed blocks. PoS is much less computationally intensive and requires vastly less energy.

CRYPTOCURRENCY

The most popular application of blockchain technology is cryptocurrency, a token (usually scarce) that is cryptographically secured and transferred. The scarcity is what assures the possibility of value and is itself an innovation of blockchain. Typically, digital objects are easily copied. As Eric Schmidt, the former CEO of Google, said,[1] "[Bitcoin] is a remarkable cryptographic achievement and the ability to create something that is not duplicable in the digital world has enormous value."

No one can post a false transaction without ownership of the corresponding account due to the *asymmetric key cryptography* protecting the accounts. You have one "public" key representing an address to receive tokens and a "private" key used to unlock and spend tokens over which you have custody. This same type of cryptography is used to protect your credit card information and data when using the Internet. A single account cannot "double spend" its tokens because the ledger keeps an audit of the balance at any given time and the faulty transaction would not clear. The ability to prevent a double spend without a central authority illustrates the primary advantage of using a blockchain to maintain the underlying ledger.

The initial cryptocurrency model is the Bitcoin blockchain, which functions almost exclusively as a payment network, with the capabilities of storing and transacting bitcoins across the globe in real time with no intermediaries or censorship. This is powerful value proposition gives bitcoin its value. Even though its network effects are strong, some competitors in the cryptocurrency space offer enhanced functionality.

THE SMART CONTRACT PLATFORM

A crucial ingredient of DeFi is a *smart contract* platform, which goes beyond a simple payments network such as Bitcoin and enhances the chain's capabilities. Ethereum is the primary example. A smart contract is code that can create and transform arbitrary data or tokens on top of the blockchain to which it belongs. Powerfully, it allows the user to trustlessly encode rules for any type of transaction and even create scarce assets with specialized functionality. Many of the clauses of traditional business agreements could be shifted to a smart contract, which not only would enumerate but also algorithmically enforce those clauses. Smart contracts go beyond finance to include gaming, data stewardship, and supply chain.

Ethereum charges a *gas fee* for every transaction – similar to how driving a car takes a certain amount of gas, which costs money. Imagine Ethereum as one giant computer with many applications (i.e., smart contracts). If people want to use the computer, they must pay for each unit of computation. A simple computation such as sending ether (ETH) requires minimal work to update a few account balances and thus has a relatively small gas fee. A complex computation involving minting tokens and checking various conditions across many contracts requires more gas and thus will have a higher fee. The gas fee may lead to a poor user experience, however. It forces agents to maintain an ETH balance to pay it and leads to worry about overpaying, underpaying, or the transaction not taking place at all. So initiatives are ongoing to eliminate gas fees from end users. There are also competitor chains that completely remove this concept of gas.

However, gas is a primary mechanism for preventing system attacks that generate an *infinite loop* of code. It is not feasible to identify malicious code of this kind before running it, a problem formally known in computer science as *the halting problem*. Suppose a car is on autopilot, stuck in full throttle with no driver. Gas acts as a limiting factor: the car will stop eventually when the gas tank empties. In the same way, gas fees secure the Ethereum blockchain by making such attacks cost-prohibitive. They incentivize highly efficient smart contract code since contracts that use fewer resources and reduce the probability of user failures have a much higher chance of being used and succeeding in the market.

On a smart contract platform, the possibilities rapidly expand beyond what developers desiring to integrate various applications can easily handle. This leads to the adoption of standard interfaces for different types of functionality. On Ethereum, these standards are called *Ethereum Request for Comments (ERC)*. The best known of these define different types of tokens that have similar behavior. ERC-20 is the standard for fungible tokens and defines an interface for tokens whose units are identical in utility and functionality.[2] It includes behavior such as transferring units and approving operators for using a certain portion of a user's balance. Another is ERC-721, the non-fungible token standard, which are unique and often used for collectibles or assets such as peer-to-peer loans. The benefit of these standards is that application developers can code for one interface and support every possible token that implements that interface. We will discuss these interfaces in more detail later on.

ORACLES

An interesting problem with blockchain protocols is that they are isolated from the world outside of their ledger. That is, the Ethereum blockchain authoritatively knows what is happening only on the Ethereum blockchain and not, for example, the level of the S&P 500 or which team won the Super Bowl. This limitation constrains applications to Ethereum native contracts and tokens, thus reducing the utility of the smart contract platform; it is generally known as the *oracle problem*. In the context of smart contract platforms, an oracle is any data source for reporting information external to the blockchain. How can we create an oracle that can authoritatively speak about off-chain information in a trust-minimized way? Many applications require an oracle, and the implementations exhibit varying degrees of centralization.

There are several implementations of oracles in various DeFi applications. A common approach is for an application to host its own oracle or hook into an existing oracle from a well-trusted platform. One Ethereum-based platform known as Chainlink[3] is designed to solve the oracle problem by using an aggregation of data sources. The Chainlink white paper[4] proposes a reputation-based system. We discuss the oracle problem later in more depth. Oracles are surely an open design question and challenge for DeFi to achieve utility beyond its own isolated chain.

STABLECOINS

A crucial shortcoming of many cryptocurrencies is excessive volatility. This adds friction to users who wish to take advantage of DeFi applications but don't have the risk-tolerance for a volatile asset like ETH. To solve this, an entire class of cryptocurrencies called stablecoins has emerged. Intended to maintain price parity with some target asset, USD, or gold, for instance, stablecoins provide the necessary consistency that investors seek to participate in many DeFi applications and allow a cryptocurrency native solution to exit positions in more volatile cryptoassets. They can even be used to provide on-chain exposure to the returns of an off-chain asset if the target asset is not native to the underlying blockchain (e.g., gold, stocks, exchange-traded funds [ETFs]). The mechanism by which the stablecoin maintains its peg varies by implementation. The three primary mechanisms are fiat-collateralized, crypto-collateralized, and non-collateralized stablecoins.

By far the largest class of stablecoins are fiat collateralized. These are backed by an off-chain reserve of the target asset. Usually they are custodied by an external entity or group of entities that undergo routine audits to verify the collateral's existence. The largest fiat-collateralized stablecoin is Tether[5] (USDT) with a market capitalization of $62 billion, making it the third largest cryptocurrency behind Bitcoin and Ethereum at time of writing. Tether also has the highest trading volume of any cryptocurrency but is not audited.[6] The second largest is USDC,[7] and its holdings of USD are regularly audited. USDC is redeemable 1:1 for USD and vice versa for no fee on Coinbase's exchange. USDT and USDC are very popular to integrate into DeFi protocols as demand for stablecoin investment opportunities is high. There is an inherent risk to these tokens, however, as they are centrally controlled and maintain the right to blacklist accounts.[8]

The second largest class of stablecoins are crypto-collateralized, meaning they are backed by an overcollateralized amount of another cryptocurrency. Their value can be hard or soft pegged to the underlying asset depending on the mechanism. With a market capitalization of $5 billion as of writing, the most popular crypto-collateralized stablecoin is DAI, created by MakerDAO[9] and and backed by ETH and other crypto assets. It is soft pegged with economic mechanisms that incentivize supply and demand to drive the price to $1. We will do a deep dive into MakerDAO and DAI in Chapter 6. Another popular crypto-collateralized stablecoin is sUSD, which is hard pegged to $1 through the Synthetix[10] network token (SNX) exchange functionality. Crypto-collateralized stablecoins have the advantages of decentralization and secured collateral. The drawback is that their scalability is limited. To mint more of the stablecoin, a user must necessarily back the issuance by an overcollateralized debt position. In some cases like DAI, a debt ceiling further limits the supply growth.

The last and perhaps most interesting class of stablecoins are non-collateralized. Not backed by any underlying asset and using algorithmic expansion and supply contraction to shift the price to the peg, they often employ a seigniorage model where the token holders in the platform receive the increase in supply when demand increases. When demand decreases and the price slips below the peg, these platforms issue bonds of some form, which entitle the holder to future expansionary supply before the token holders receive their share. This mechanism works almost identically to the central bank associated with fiat currencies, with the caveat that these platforms have an explicit goal of pegging the price rather than funding government spending or other economic goals. A noteworthy early example of an algorithmic stablecoin is Basis,[11] which had to close due to regulatory hurdles. Current examples of algorithmic stablecoins include Ampleforth (AMPL)[12] and Empty Set Dollar (ESD).[13] The drawback to non-collateralized stablecoins is that they have a lack of inherent underlying value backing the exchange of their token. In contractions, this can lead to "bank runs," in which many holders are left with large sums of the token that are no longer worth the peg price.

There is still much work to be done – and regulatory hurdles to overcome – in creating a decentralized stablecoin that both scales efficiently and is resistant to collapse in contractions.[14] Stablecoins are an important component of DeFi infrastructure because they allow users to benefit from the functionality of the applications without risking unnecessary price volatility.

DECENTRALIZED APPLICATIONS

As mentioned earlier, dApps are a critical DeFi ingredient. dApps are like traditional software applications except they live on a decentralized smart contract platform. The primary benefit of these applications is their *permissionlessness* and *censorship resistance*. Anyone can use them, and no single body controls them. A separate but related concept is a *decentralized autonomous organization (DAO)*, which has its rules of operation encoded in smart contracts that determine who can execute what behavior or upgrade. It is common for a DAO to have some kind of *governance token,* which gives an owner some percentage of the vote on future outcomes. We will explore governance in much more detail later.

IV

DeFi PRIMITIVES

Now that the DeFi infrastructure has been discussed in detail, this chapter describes the primitive financial actions that developers can use and combine to create complex dApps and the advantages each action may have over its centralized counterparts.

TRANSACTIONS

Ethereum transactions are the atoms of DeFi (and Ethereum as a whole). Transactions involve sending data or ETH (or other tokens) from one address to another. All Ethereum interactions, including each of the primitives discussed in this section, begin with a transaction. Therefore, how transactions work is an integral part of understanding Ethereum in particular and DeFi in general.

In Ethereum, there are two types of addresses: the *externally owned account* (EOA) and an address of a *contract account.* Transactions sent to an EOA can only transfer ETH.[1] In Bitcoin, all addresses are EOA. In Ethereum, when data is sent to a contract account, the data are used to execute code in that contract. The transaction may or may not have an accompanying ETH payment for use by the contract.

A single transaction starts with an end user from an EOA but can interact with many dApps (or any Ethereum smart contract) before completing. The transaction starts by interacting with a single contract, which will enumerate all the intermediate steps in the transaction required within the contract body.

Clauses in a smart contract can cause a transaction to fail and thereby revert all previous steps of the transaction; as a result, transactions are *atomic.* Atomicity is a critical feature of transactions because funds can move between many contracts (i.e., exchange hands) with the knowledge and security that if one of the conditions is not met, the contract terms reset as if the money never left the starting point.

Remember that transactions have a gas fee, which varies based on the complexity of the transaction. When, for example, ETH is used to compensate a miner for including and executing a transaction, the gas fee is relatively low. Longer or more data-intensive transactions cost more gas. If a transaction reverts for any reason, or runs out of gas, the sender forfeits all gas used until that point. Forfeiture protects the miners who, without this provision, could fall prey to large volumes of failed transactions for which they would not receive payment.

The gas price is determined by the market and effectively creates an auction for inclusion in the next Ethereum block. Higher gas fees signal higher demand and therefore generally receive higher priority for inclusion.

A technical aside about transactions is that they are posted to a *memory pool,* or *mempool,* before they are added to a block. Miners monitor these posted transactions, add them to their own mempool, and share the transaction with other miners to be included in the next available block. If the gas price offered by the transaction is uncompetitive relative to other transactions in the mempool, the transaction is deferred to a future block.

Any actor can see transactions in the mempool by running or communicating with mining nodes. This visibility can even allow for advanced front-running and other competitive techniques that aid the miner in profiting from trading activity. In contrast to traditional centralized markets, this front-running is legal given that all information is public. If miners see a transaction in the mempool, they could profit from it either by executing it themselves or front-running it and is incentivized to do so if they are lucky enough to win the block. Any occurrence of direct execution is known as *miner extractable value* (MEV), which is a drawback to the proof-of-work model. Certain strategies, such as obfuscating transactions, can mitigate MEV, thus hiding from miners how they might profit from the transactions.

FUNGIBLE TOKENS

Fungible tokens are a cornerstone of the value proposition of Ethereum and DeFi. Any Ethereum developer can create a token divisible to a certain decimal granularity and with units that are all identical and interchangeable. By way of example, USD is a fungible asset because one $100 bill is equivalent to a hundred $1 bills. As we mentioned in Chapter 3, the Ethereum blockchain token interface is ERC-20.[2] An interface from an application developer's perspective is the minimum required set of functionalities. When a token implements the ERC-20 interface, any application that generically handles the defined functionality can instantly and seamlessly integrate with the token. Using ERC-20 and similar interfaces, application developers can confidently support tokens that do not yet exist.

The ERC-20 interface defines the following core functionality:

- totalSupply() – read the token's total supply
- balanceOf(account) – read the balance of the token for a particular account
- transfer(recipient address, amount) – send "amount" tokens from the transaction sender to "recipient address"
- transferFrom(sender address, recipient address, amount) – send "amount" tokens from the balance of tokens held at "sender address" to "recipient address"

- approve(spender, amount) – allows "spender" to spend "amount" tokens on behalf of the account owner
- allowance(owner address, spender address) – returns the number of tokens the "spender address" can spend on behalf of the "owner address"

The contract will reject transfers involving insufficient balances or unauthorized spending. The first four functions – reading supply, balances, and sending tokens – are intuitive and expected. The last two functions – approve and allowance – are critical to understanding the power of the ERC-20 interface. Without these functions, users would be limited to directly transferring tokens to and from accounts. With approval functionality, contracts (or trusted accounts) can be whitelisted to act as custodians for a user's tokens without directly holding the token balance. This widens the scope of possible applications because users retain full custody before an approved spender executes a transaction.

There are three main ERC-20 token main categories, but tokens can be in more than one at the same time.

Equity Token

An equity token – not to be confused with equities or stocks in the traditional finance sense – represents ownership of an underlying asset or pool of assets. The units must be fungible so that each corresponds to an identical share in the pool. For example, suppose a token TKN has a total fixed supply of 10,000 and corresponds to an ETH pool of 100 ETH held in a smart contract. The smart contract stipulates that for every unit of TKN it receives, it will return a pro rata amount of ETH, fixing the exchange ratio at 100 TKN/1 ETH. We can extend the example so that the pool has a variable amount of ETH. Suppose the ETH in the pool increases at 5 percent per year by some other mechanism. Now, 100 TKN would represent 1 ETH plus a 5 percent perpetuity cash flow of ETH. The market can use this information to accurately price the value of TKN.

In actual equity tokens, the pools of assets can contain much more complex mechanics, going beyond a static pool or fixed rates of increase. The possibilities are limited only by what can be encoded into a smart contract. Chapter 6 examines a contract with variable interest-rate mechanics (Compound tokens) and a contract that owns a multi-asset pool with a complex fee structure (Uniswap) and also explains Set Protocol, which defines a standard interface for creating equity tokens with static or dynamic holdings.

Utility Tokens

Utility tokens are in many ways a catchall bucket, although they do have a clear definition: fungible tokens required to use some functionality of a smart contract system or with an intrinsic value proposition defined by their respective smart contract system. In many cases, utility tokens drive the economics of a system, creating scarcity or incentives where intended by the developers. In some cases, ETH could be used instead, but utility tokens allow systems to accrue and maintain decoupled economic value from Ethereum as a whole. For example, a system with algorithmically varied supply would require a distinct utility token. The mechanics are discussed in more depth later in this chapter.

Utility tokens can be used as collateral (e.g., SNX), as a placeholder for reputation or stake (e.g., REP, LINK), to maintain stable value relative to underlying or peg (e.g., DAI, Synthetix Synth), and to pay application-specific fees (e.g., ZRX, DAI, LINK). The latter includes all stablecoins, regardless of whether the stablecoin is fiat or crypto-collateralized or algorithmic. In the case of USDC, a fiat-collateralized stablecoin, the utility token operates as its own system without any additional smart contract infrastructure to support its value. The value of USDC arises from the promise of redemption for USD by its backing companies, including Coinbase.

Far more possibilities exist for utility tokens than the few we have mentioned here. Innovation will expand this category as novel economic and technical mechanisms emerge.

Governance Tokens

Governance and equity tokens both represent percentage ownership: *equity* refers to the share of assets and governance to voting rights. We start by motivating the types of changes on which owners can vote.

Many smart contracts have embedded clauses stipulating how the system can change; for instance, allowed changes could include adjusting parameters, adding new components, or even altering the functionality of existing components. The ability of the system to change is a powerful proposition given the possibility that the contract a user interacts with today could change tomorrow. In some cases, only developer admins, who encode special privileges for themselves, can control changes to the platform.

Any platform with admin-controlled functionality is not truly DeFi because of the admins' centralized control. A contract without the capacity for change is necessarily rigid, however, and has no way to adapt to bugs in the code or changing economic or technical conditions. For this reason, many platforms strive for a decentralized upgrade process, often mediated by a governance token.

The owners of a governance token would have pro rata voting rights for implementing any change allowed by the smart contracts that govern the platform. Voting mechanisms and *decentralized autonomous organizations* (DAOs) are covered in Chapter 5.

A governance token can be implemented in many ways: with a static, an inflationary, or even a deflationary supply. A static supply is straightforward: purchased tokens would correspond directly to a certain percentage control of the vote. The current implementation of the MKR token for MakerDAO has a generally static supply. Chapter 6 delves into MakerDAO and its implementation.

Many platforms issue the governance token via an inflation schedule that incentivizes people to use particular features of the platform, ensuring the governance token is distributed directly to them. Compound, for example, takes an inflationary implementation approach with its COMP token (see Chapter 6). A deflationary approach would likely consist of using the governance token also as a utility token to pay fees to the platform, which would be burned, or removed, from the supply rather than going to a specific entity. The MKR token of MakerDAO used to be burned in this manner in an older version of the platform.

NON-FUNGIBLE TOKENS

As the name suggests, the units of a non-fungible token (NFT) are not equal to those of other tokens.

NFT Standard

On Ethereum, the ERC-721[3] standard defines non-fungibility. It is like ERC-20, except that rather than all IDs being stored as a single balance, each unit has its own unique ID that can be linked to additional metadata, which differentiate it from other tokens stemming from the same contract. Under the balanceOf(address) method, the total number of NFTs in the given contract that the address owns is returned. An additional method, ownerOf(id), returns the address of the owner of a specific token, referenced by its ID. Another important difference is that ERC-20 allows for the partial approval of an operator's token balances, whereas

ERC-721 uses an all-or-nothing approach. An operator approved to use the NFTs can move any of them.

NFTs have interesting applications in DeFi. Their alternate name, *deeds*, implies their use case as representing unique ownership of unitary assets; an example could be ownership of a particular peer-to-peer loan with its own rates and terms. The asset could then be transferred and sold via the ERC-721 interface. Another use case might be to represent a share in a lottery, in which tickets could be considered non-fungible because only one or a limited number will win and the remainder are worthless. NFTs also have a strong use case in their ability to bridge financial and non-financial use cases via *collectibles* (e.g., a token could represent ownership of a piece of art, a video, music, or even a tweet, for example). NFTs can also represent scarce items in a gaming environment or other network and retain economic value in secondary markets for NFTs.

Multitoken Standard

ERC-20 and ERC-721 tokens require an individual contract and address deployed to the blockchain, which can be cumbersome for systems with many closely related tokens – possibly even a mix of fungible and non-fungible. The ERC-1155[4] standard resolves this complexity by defining a multi-token model in which the contract holds balances for a variable number, including fungible and non-fungible. The standard also allows for batch reading and transfers, which saves on gas costs and leads to a smoother user experience. Under ERC-1155 and similar to ERC-721, operators are approved for all supported tokens in a binary all-or-none fashion.

CUSTODY

A critical DeFi primitive is the ability to escrow or custody funds directly in a smart contract. This is distinct from the situation in ERC-20 when operators are approved to transfer a user's balance. In that case, the user still retains custody of their funds and could transfer the balance anytime or revoke the contract's approval. When a smart contract has full custody over funds, it presents the possibility for new capabilities (and additional primitives), including:

- Retaining fees and disbursing incentives
- Facilitation of token swaps
- Market making of a bonding curve
- Collateralized loans
- Auctions
- Insurance funds

To effectively custody tokens, a contract must be programmed to handle the interface of the corresponding type, which would be ERC-20 for fungible and ERC-721 for non-fungible. The contract could generically handle all tokens of that interface or of a specific subset only. When a token is sent to a contract, it could become permanently custodied if the contract has no encoded mechanism for releasing the token's funds. To mitigate this potential problem, safety checks are often embedded in the token transfer to verify whether the contract is registered to support it.

SUPPLY ADJUSTMENT

Supply adjustment applies specifically to fungible tokens and the ability to create (*mint*) and reduce (*burn*) supply via a smart contract. We will now explore these basic primitives along with a more complex system known as a *bonding curve*.

Burn: Reduce Supply

Burning a token means removing it from circulation and can be done in two ways: (1) manually send it to an unowned Ethereum address; or (2) even more efficiently, create a contract that is incapable of spending it. Either approach renders the burned tokens unusable, although the decrease in circulating supply would not be "known" by the token contract. Burning is analogous to the destruction or irreversible loss of currency in the traditional finance (i.e., where worn-out paper currency is burned and replaced with freshly printed currency). In practice, ETH or ERC-20 tokens have frequently and accidently been burned using both forms; checksumming addresses[5] and registering contracts[6] are in place to prevent this from happening.

More common and useful is the ability to intentionally burn tokens as a part of the smart contract design. Here are some example use cases for burning tokens algorithmically:

- Represent exiting of a pool and redemption of underlying (common in equity tokens like cTokens for Compound that are discussed in Chapter 6)
- Increase scarcity to drive the price up (e.g., AAVE in Chapter 6, Seigniorage Stablecoin models like Basis/ESD)
- Penalize bad acting

Mint: Increase Supply

The flip side of burning is *minting*, which increases the number of tokens in circulation. Contrary to burning, there is no mechanism for accidentally or manually minting tokens. Any mint mechanics have to be directly encoded into the smart contract mechanism. There are many use cases for minting as it can incentivize a wider range of user behavior. Here are some examples:

- Represent entering a pool and acquiring corresponding ownership share (common in equity tokens like cTokens for Compound)
- Decrease scarcity (increase supply) to drive the price downward (seigniorage Stablecoin models like Basis/ESD)
- Reward user behavior

Rewarding user behavior with increases in supply (*inflationary rewards*) has become a common practice to encourage actions such as supplying liquidity or using a particular platform. Consequently, many users engage in *yield farming*, taking actions to seek the highest possible rewards. Platforms can bootstrap their networks by issuing a token with an additional value proposition in the network. Users can keep the token and deploy it in the context of the network or sell it for a profit. Either way, employing tokens in a platform usually increases activity.

Bonding Curve: Pricing Supply

Adjusting supply up and down contractually defines a bonding curve: the price relationship between the token supply and a corresponding asset used to purchase the tokens. In most implementations, investors sell back to the curve using the same price relationship. The relationship is defined as a mathematical function or as an algorithm with several clauses.

To illustrate, let TKN denote the price of a token denominated in ETH (which could be any fungible cryptoasset), and let S represent the supply. The simplest possible bonding curve would be TKN = 1 (or any constant). This relationship – TKN backed by a constant ratio of ETH – enforces that TKN is pegged to the price of ETH. The next-level bonding curve could be a simple linear bonding curve, where m and b represent the slope and intercept, respectively, in a standard linear function, Price(TKN) = $mS + b$. If $m = 1$ and $b = 0$, the first TKN would cost 1 ETH, the second would cost 2 ETH, and so on. A monotonically increasing bonding curve rewards early investors because any incremental demand

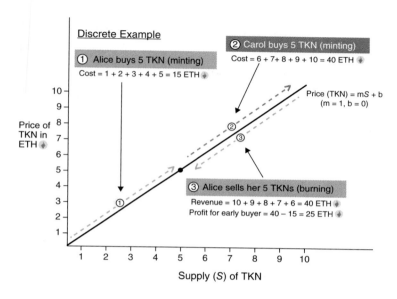

Figure 4.1 Linear bonding curve

beyond their purchase price would allow them to sell back against the curve at a higher price point (Figure 4.1).

The mechanics of a bonding curve are relatively straightforward. The curve can be represented as a single smart contract with options for purchasing and selling the underlying token. The token to be sold can have either an uncapped supply with the bonding curve as an authorized minter or a predetermined maximum supply that is escrowed in the bonding curve contract. As users purchase the token, the bonding curve escrows the incoming funding for the point in the future when they may want to sell back against the curve.

The growth rate of the bonding curve is important in determining users' performance. A linear growth rate would generously reward early users if the token grows to a sufficiently large supply. An even more extreme return could result from a superlinear growth rate (Figure 4.2), such as TKN = S^2. The first token would cost 1 ETH, and the hundredth would cost 10,000 ETH. In practice, most projects would use a sublinear growth rate or a logistic function (Figure 4.3) that converges on an upper bounded price.

A bonding curve can have a different price curve for buyers and for sellers (Figure 4.4). The selling curve could have a lower growth rate or intercept than the buying curve.

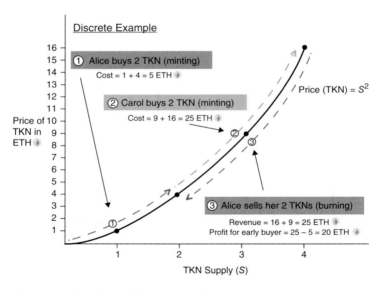

Figure 4.2   Superlinear bonding curve

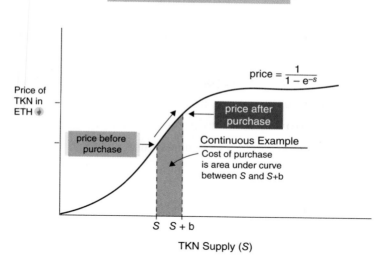

Figure 4.3   Logistic/sigmoid bonding curve

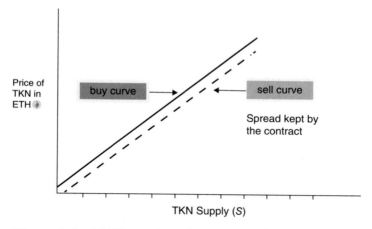

Figure 4.4   Different bonding curves for purchases and sales

The spread between the curves would be the value (in this case ETH) accrued to the smart contract and could represent a fee for usage or used to finance more complex functionality within the system. As long as the contract maintains sufficient collateral to sell back down the entire sell curve, the contract is capitalized and able to fulfill any sell demand.

INCENTIVES

Incentives within cryptoeconomic systems including DeFi are extremely important in encouraging desired (positive incentive) and discouraging undesired (negative incentive) user behaviors. The term *incentive* is quite broad, but we narrow our discussion to direct token payments or fees. We will look at two different categories of incentives: (1) *staked incentives,* which apply to a balance of tokens custodied in a smart contract; and (2) *direct incentives,* which apply to users within the system who do not have a custodied balance.

Mechanisms in the contract determine the source of any reward funds and the destination for fees. Reward funds can be issued through inflation or by minting or can be custodied in the smart contract. Funds removed as a fee can be burned or retained in the smart contract's custody. Reward funds can also be issued as a direct incentive to the platform's participants or raised through an auction to repay a debt. A mechanism might instigate a burn to reduce the supply of a particular token to increase price pressure.

Staking Rewards

A *staking reward* is a positive incentive by which users receive a bonus in their token balance based on the amount of capital they have contributed to the system. Options for customization include applying a minimum threshold to all staked balances on a pro rata basis, either a fixed or pro rata payout, and a token that is the same or different from the staked one.

The Compound Protocol (which is discussed in Chapter 6) issues staking rewards on user balances that are custodied in a borrowing or lending position. These rewards are paid in a separate token (COMP) funded by custodied COMP, which has a fixed supply, and applied to all staked balances on a pro rata basis. The Synthetix Protocol issues staking rewards on staked SNX, its Protocol token with unlimited supply. The rewards are paid in SNX, funded by inflation, and issued only if the user meets a minimum collateralization ratio threshold.

Slashing (Staking Penalties)

Slashing is the removal of a portion of a user's staked balance, thereby creating a negative staked incentive, and occurs as the result of an undesirable event. A *slashing condition* is a mechanism that triggers a slashing and can be customized by partial or complete removal of funds, liquidation triggered by undercollateralization, detectable malicious user behavior, and necessary contraction triggered by a change in market conditions.

In the forthcoming discussion on collateralized loans, we will illustrate the common slashing mechanism of *liquidation*, in which potential agents receive an incentive to offload collateral by auction or direct sales and any remaining funds stay with the original owner. An example of slashing due to market changes not related to debt is an algorithmic stablecoin. This system might directly reduce a user's token balance when the price depreciates to return the supply-weighted price to, say, $1.

Direct Rewards and Keepers

Direct rewards are positive incentives that include payments or fees associated with user actions. As we mentioned already, all Ethereum interactions begin with a transaction, and all transactions begin with an externally owned account. An EOA, whether controlled by a human user or an off-chain bot, is (importantly) off chain, and thus autonomous response to market conditions is either expensive (costs gas) or technically infeasible. As a result, no transaction happens automatically on Ethereum without being purposely set in motion.

The classic example of a transaction that must be set in motion is when a collateralized debt position becomes undercollateralized. This use case does not automatically trigger a liquidation; the EOA must trigger it and generally receive a direct incentive to do so. The contract then evaluates the conditions and liquidates or updates if everything is as expected.

A *keeper* is a class of EOA incentivized either with a flat fee or percentage to perform an action in a DeFi protocol or other dApp. Thus, autonomous monitoring can be outsourced off chain, creating robust economies and new profit opportunities. Keeper rewards may also be structured as an auction to ensure competition and best price. Keeper auctions are very competitive because the information available in the system is almost entirely public. A side effect of direct rewards for keepers is that gas prices can inflate due to the competition for these rewards. That is, more keeper activity generates additional demand for transactions, which in turn increases the price of gas.

Fees

Fees are typically a funding mechanism for the features of the system or platform. They can be flat or percentage based, depending on the desired incentive. Fees can be imposed as a direct negative incentive or can be accrued on staked balances. Accrued fees must have an associated staked balance to ensure the user pays them. Because of the pseudonymous anonymous nature of Ethereum accounts – all that is known about an Ethereum user is their wallet balance and interactions with various contracts on Ethereum – the imposition of fees is a design challenge. If the smart contract is open to any Ethereum account, the only way to guarantee enforcement is for all debts to be backed by staked on-chain collateral which is transparent. The challenges created by anonymity make other mechanisms such as reputation, unreliable compared to staked balances.[7]

SWAP

A swap is simply the exchange of one type of token for another. The key benefit of swapping in DeFi is that it is atomic and non-custodial. Funds can be custodied in a smart contract with withdrawal rights that can be exercised anytime before the swap is completed. The swap executes only when the exchange conditions are agreed to and met by all parties and are enforced by the smart contract. If any condition is not met, the entire transaction is canceled and all parties retain their custodied funds. A platform that facilitates token swapping on Ethereum in a non-custodial fashion is a *decentralized exchange* (DEX). There are two primary mechanisms for DEX liquidity: an order-matching approach and an *Automated Market Maker* (AMM).

Order-Book Matching

Order-book matching is a system in which all parties must agree on the swap exchange rate. Market makers can post bids and asks to a DEX, and allow takers to fill the quotes at the previously agreed on price. Until the offer is taken, the market maker retains the right to remove the offer or update the exchange rate as market conditions change.

The order-matching approach is expensive and inefficient because each update requires an on-chain transaction. An insurmountable inefficiency with an order-book matching is that both counterparties must be willing and able to exchange at the agreed on rate for the trade to execute. This requirement creates limitations for many smart contract applications in which demand for exchange liquidity cannot be dependent on a counterparty's availability. An innovative alternative is an AMM.

Automated Market Makers

An AMM is a smart contract that holds assets on both sides of a trading pair and continuously quotes a price for buying and for selling. Based on executed purchases and sales, the contract updates the asset size behind the bid and the ask and uses this ratio to define its pricing function. The contract can also account for more complex data than relative bid–ask size when determining price. From the contract's perspective, the price should be risk-neutral where it is indifferent to buying or selling.

A naive AMM might set a fixed price ratio between two assets. With a fixed price ratio, when the market price shifts between the assets, the more valuable asset would be drained from the AMM and arbitraged on another exchange where trading is occurring at the market price. The AMM should have a pricing function that can converge to an asset's market price. That is, the pricing function makes it more expensive to purchase the asset from the trading pair as the ratio of the asset to others in the contract decreases.

The major benefits of an AMM are that it is always available and that a traditional counterparty is not necessary to execute a trade. These provisions are very important for smart contracts and DeFi development because of the guarantee that a user can exchange assets at any moment if necessary. Users maintain custody of their funds until they complete the trade; hence, counterparty risk is zero. An additional benefit is *composable liquidity*, which means any exchange contract can plug into the liquidity and exchange rates of any other exchange contract. AMMs make this particularly easy because of their guaranteed availability and their allowance of one-sided trading against the contract. Composable liquidity correlates comfortably with the concept of DeFi Legos (which we will discuss later).

One drawback to an AMM is *impermanent loss*: the opportunity–cost dynamic between offering assets for exchange and holding the underlying assets to potentially profit from the price movement. The loss is impermanent because it can be recovered if the price reverts to its original level. To illustrate, consider two assets, A and B, each initially worth 1 ETH as in Figure 4.5. The AMM contract holds identical quantities of 100 of each asset and naively offers both at a fixed exchange rate of 1:1. We use ETH as the unit of account to track the contract's return on its holdings and any impermanent loss. At the given balances and market exchange rates, the contract has 200 ETH in escrow. Suppose asset B's price appreciates to 4 ETH in the wider market and asset A's price appreciates to 2 ETH. Arbitrageurs exchange all of asset B

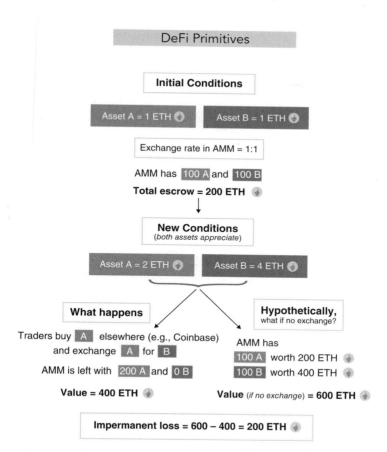

Figure 4.5 **The mechanics of automated market makers**

in the contract for asset A because asset B is more valuable. The contract then holds 200 of asset A worth 400 ETH. In this case, the contract's return is 100 percent.

If, however, the contract does not sell asset B, the contract's value would be 600 ETH. The contract has an impermanent loss equal to 200 ETH, the difference between 600 ETH and 400 ETH. If the contract's holdings return to parity between assets A and B, the impermanent loss disappears. If the goal for liquidity held in the contract is profit, any fees charged must exceed the amount of the impermanent loss.

Impermanent loss occurs for any shift in price and liquidity because the contract is structured to sell the appreciating asset and to buy the depreciating asset. An important feature of impermanent loss is *path independence*. In our example, it is irrelevant whether 1 or 100 traders consumed all the liquidity. The final exchange rate and contract asset ratios yield the same impermanent loss regardless of the number of trades or the direction of the trades. Because of path independence, impermanent loss is minimized on trading pairs that have correlated prices (*mean-reverting pairs*). Thus, stablecoin trading pairs are particularly attractive for AMMs.

COLLATERALIZED LOANS

Debt and lending are perhaps the most important financial mechanisms that exist in DeFi and, more generally, in traditional finance. On one hand, these mechanisms are a powerful tool for efficiently allocating capital, increasing return-bearing risk exposure, and expanding economic growth. On the other hand, excess debt in the system can cause instability, potentially leading to large economic and market contractions. These benefits and risks are amplified in DeFi because the counterparties share an adversarial and integrated environment. Platforms are increasingly interdependent, and a debt-fueled collapse in one part of the system can quickly contaminate all connected protocols – and expand outward.

Any loan of non-zero duration (e.g., foreshadowing flash loan) must be backed by an equivalent or excess amount of collateral. Requiring collateral contractually prevents a counterparty from defaulting. An uncollateralized mechanism raises the risk that a counterparty could steal funds, especially in an open and anonymous system such as Ethereum. A risk of overcollateralized positions is that the collateral becomes less valuable than the debt, leading to a foreclosure without an option for recovery. Therefore, more volatile types of collateral require larger collateralization ratios to mitigate this risk.

We have already mentioned the mechanism of liquidation, and now we will explain it in detail. To avoid liquidation, it is imperative that debt remain overcollateralized by a margin sufficiently large that moderate price volatility does not place the collateral value in jeopardy. Smart contracts commonly define a minimum collateralization threshold below which the collateral can be liquidated and the position closed. The collateral could be auctioned or directly sold on a DEX, likely with an AMM, at the market price.

As stated already, positions in the Ethereum blockchain cannot be liquidated automatically, so an incentive is needed and often takes the form of a percentage fee allocated to an external keeper who is able to liquidate the position and collect the reward. Any remaining collateral is left to the original holder of the position. In some cases, the system will leave all remaining collateral to the keeper as a stronger incentive. Because the penalty for liquidation is high and most collateral types are volatile, platforms generally allow users to top up their collateral to maintain healthy collateralization ratios.

An interesting implication of collateralized loans and token supply adjustment is that collateralization can back the value of a synthetic token. The synthetic token is an asset created and funded by a debt, which has the requirement to repay the synthetic token to reclaim the collateral. The synthetic token can have a utility mechanism or represent a complex financial derivative, such as an option or bond (e.g., Synthetix Synth and Yield yToken; see Chapter 6). A stablecoin that tracks the price of an underlying asset can also be a synthetic token of this type (e.g., MakerDAO DAI; see Chapter 6).

FLASH (UNCOLLATERALIZED) LOANS

A financial primitive that uniquely exists in DeFi and dramatically broadens certain types of financial access is a *flash loan*. In traditional finance, a loan is an instrument designed to efficiently allocate excess capital from a person or entity who wishes to employ it (lender) to a person or entity who needs capital to fund a project or to consume (borrower). A lender is compensated for providing the capital and bearing the risk of default by the interest amount charged over the life of the loan. The interest rate is typically higher the longer the duration of the loan because the longer time to repay exposes the lender to greater risk that the borrower may default.

Reversing the concept leads to the conclusion that shorter-term loans should be less risky and therefore require less compensation for the lender. A flash loan is an instantaneous loan paid back within the same transaction. A flash loan is similar to an overnight loan in traditional finance but with a crucial difference: repayment is required within the transaction and enforced by the smart contract.

A thorough understanding of an Ethereum transaction is important for understanding how flash loans work. One clause in the transaction is vital: if the loan is not repaid with required interest by the end of the transaction, the whole process reverts to the state before any money ever left the lender's account. In other words, either the user successfully employs the loan for the desired use case and completely repays it in the transaction, or the transaction fails and everything resets as if the user had not borrowed any money.

Flash loans essentially have zero counterparty risk or duration risk. However, there is always smart contract risk (e.g., a flaw in the contract design; see Chapter 7). Flash loans allow a user to take advantage of arbitrage opportunities or to refinance loans without pledging collateral. This capability allows anyone in the world to have access to opportunities that typically require very large amounts of capital investment. In time, we will see similar innovations that could not exist in the world of traditional finance.

V

PROBLEMS
DeFi SOLVES

This chapter addresses DeFi's concrete solutions to the five flaws of traditional finance: inefficiency, limited access, opacity, centralized control, and lack of interoperability.

INEFFICIENCY

The first of the five flaws of traditional finance is inefficiency. DeFi can handle financial transactions with high volumes of assets and low friction that would generally be a large organizational burden for traditional finance. It does this by creating dApps: reusable smart contracts designed to execute a specific financial operation and available to any user who seeks that type of service, for example, to execute a put option, regardless of the size of the transaction. A user can largely self-serve within the parameters of the smart contract and of the blockchain the application lives on. In the case of Ethereum-based DeFi, the contracts can be used by anyone who pays the flat gas fee, currently around $3 for a transfer and $12 for a dApp feature such as leveraging against collateral. Once deployed, these contracts continually provide their service with near-zero organizational overhead.

Keepers

Introduced in Chapter 4, keepers are external participants directly incentivized to provide a service to DeFi protocols, such as monitoring positions to safeguard that they are sufficiently collateralized or triggering state updates for various functions. To ensure that a dApp's benefits and services are optimally priced, keeper rewards are often structured as an auction. Pure, open competition provides value to DeFi platforms by guaranteeing users pay the market price for the services they need.

Forking

Another concept that also incentivizes efficiency is a *fork*. In the context of open-source code, this occurs when the code is copied and reused with upgrades or enhancements layered on top. A common fork in blockchain protocols is formed when they are referenced in two parallel currencies and chains. Doing so creates competition at the protocol level and creates the best possible smart contract platform. Not only is the code of the entire Ethereum blockchain public and forkable, but each DeFi dApp built on top of Ethereum is as well. Should inefficient or suboptimal DeFi applications exist, the code can be easily copied, improved, and redeployed through forking. Forking and its benefits arise from the open nature of DeFi and blockchains.

Forking creates an interesting challenge to DeFi platforms, namely, *vampirism*: an exact or near-carbon copy of a DeFi platform designed to poach liquidity or users by offering larger incentives than the platform it is copying. Users might be attracted to the higher potential reward for the same functionality, which would cause a reduction in usage and liquidity on the initial platform.

If the inflationary rewards are flawed, with prolonged use the clone could perhaps collapse after a large asset bubble or could select closer-to-optimal models and replace the original platform. Vampirism is not an inherent risk or flaw but rather a complicating factor arising from the pure competition and openness of DeFi. The selection process will eventually give rise to more robust financial infrastructure with optimal efficiency.

LIMITED ACCESS

As smart contract platforms move to more scalable implementations, user friction falls, enabling a wide range of users and thus mitigating the second flaw of traditional finance:

limited access. DeFi gives large, underserved groups like the global unbanked population and small businesses that employ substantial portions of the workforce (e.g., nearly 50 percent in the United States) direct access to financial services. The resulting impact on the entire global economy should be strongly positive. Even consumers who have access to traditional financial services such as bank accounts, mortgages, and credit cards cannot get products with the most competitive pricing and most favorable terms because they are restricted to large institutions. DeFi allows all users access to the entirety of its financial infrastructure, regardless of their wealth or geographic location.

Yield Farming

Yield farming provides access to many who need financial services but whom traditional finance leaves behind. It provides users with inflationary or contract-funded rewards for staking capital or using a protocol, which are then payable in the same underlying asset the user holds or in a distinct asset such as a governance token. Any user can participate, staking an amount of any size – regardless of how small – and receiving a proportional reward. This capability is particularly powerful in the case of governance tokens. A user of a protocol that issues a governance token via yield farming becomes a partial owner of the platform through the issued token. A rare occurrence in traditional finance, this process is a common and celebrated way to give ownership of the platform to the people who use and benefit from it.

Initial DeFi Offering

An interesting consequence of yield farming is that a user can create an *initial DeFi offering* (IDO) by market making their own Uniswap (discussed in the next chapter) trading pair. They can set the initial exchange rate by becoming the first liquidity provider on the pair. Suppose the user's token is called DFT and has a total supply of 2 million. They can make each DFT worth 0.10 USDC by opening the market with 1 million DFT and 100,000 USDC. Any ERC-20 token holder can purchase DFT, which drives up the price. As the only liquidity provider, the user also receives all the trading fees. In this way, they can get their token immediate access to as many users as possible. The method sets an artificial price floor for the token if the user controls the supply outside of the amount supplied to the Uniswap market and, as such, inhibits price discovery. The trade-offs of an IDO should be weighed as an option, or strategy, for a user's token distribution.

IDOs democratize access to DeFi in two ways. First, an IDO allows a project to list on high-traffic DeFi exchanges that do not have barriers to entry beyond the initial capital. Second, an IDO allows a user access to the best new projects immediately after the project lists.

OPACITY

The third drawback of traditional finance is opacity. DeFi elegantly solves this problem through the open and contractual nature of agreements. We will explore how smart contracts and tokenization improve transparency within DeFi.

Smart Contracts

Smart contracts provide an immediate benefit in terms of transparency. All parties are aware of the capitalization of their counterparties and, to the extent required, can see how funds will be deployed. They can each read the contract, agree on the terms, and eliminate any ambiguity. This transparency substantially eases the threat of legal burdens and brings peace of mind to smaller players who, in the current environment of traditional finance, could be abused by powerful counterparties through delaying or even completely withholding their end of a financial agreement. Realistically, the average consumer does not understand the contract code but can rely on the open-source nature of the platform, the existence of code audits (discussed later) and the wisdom of the crowd to feel secure. Overall, DeFi mitigates counterparty risk and thus creates a host of efficiencies not present under traditional finance.

DeFi participants are accountable for acting in accordance with the terms of the contracts they use. One mechanism for ensuring the appropriate behavior is *staking*, in which a cryptoasset is escrowed into a contract and released to the appropriate counterparty only after the terms are met or is returned to the original holder. Parties can be required to stake on any claims or interactions they make. Staking enforces agreements by imposing a tangible penalty for the misbehaving side and a tangible reward for the counterparty, the latter of which should be as good as or even better than the outcome of the original terms of the contract. These transparent incentive structures provide much more secure and more obvious guarantees than traditional financial agreements.

Another type of smart contract in DeFi that improves transparency is a *token contract*, which allows users to know exactly how many tokens are in the system and the parameters of inflation and deflation.

CENTRALIZED CONTROL

The fourth flaw of traditional finance is the strong control exerted by governments and large institutions that hold a virtual monopoly over elements such as the money supply, rate of inflation, and access to the best investment opportunities. DeFi upends this centralized control by relinquishing control to open protocols with transparent and immutable properties. The community of stakeholders or even a predetermined algorithm can control a DeFi dApp's parameter, such as the inflation rate. If a dApp contains special privileges for an administrator, all users are aware of the privileges, and any user can readily create a less centralized competitor.

The open-source ethos of blockchain and the public nature of all smart contracts assures that flaws and inefficiencies in a DeFi project can be readily identified and "forked away" by users who copy and improve the flawed project. Consequently, DeFi strives to design protocols that naturally and elegantly incentivize stakeholders and maintain a healthy equilibrium through careful mechanism design. Naturally, there are trade-offs in having and not having a centralized party. Centralized control allows for radically decisive action in a crisis, which may or may not be the appropriate reaction. The path to decentralizing finance will certainly involve growing pains because of the challenges in pre-planning for every eventuality and economic nuance. Ultimately, however, the transparency and security a decentralized approach brings will lead to robust protocols that can become trusted financial infrastructure for a global user base.

Decentralized Autonomous Organization

In a *decentralized autonomous organization* (DAO), the rules of operation are encoded in smart contracts that determine who can execute what behavior or upgrade. It is common for a DAO to have some kind of *governance token*, which gives an owner some percentage of the vote on future outcomes. We will explore governance in much more detail later.

LACK OF INTEROPERABILITY

We will now touch on how DeFi solves for the lack of interoperability that exists in traditional finance. Traditional financial products are difficult to integrate, generally requiring at minimum a wire transfer and many cases unable to be recombined. The possibilities for DeFi are substantial, and new innovations continue to grow exponentially, fueled by how easy it is to compose DeFi products. Once a base infrastructure has been established – for example, to create a synthetic asset – any new protocols allowing for borrowing and lending can be applied. A higher layer would allow for attainment of leverage on top of borrowed assets. Such composability can continue in an increasing number of directions as new platforms arise. For this reason, *DeFi Legos* is an analogy often used to describe the act of combining existing protocols into a new protocol. The next section discusses tokenization and networked liquidity, which are advantages to this composability.

Tokenization

Tokenization is a critical way DeFi platforms integrate. Take, for example, a percentage ownership stake in a private commercial real estate venture. It would be quite difficult in traditional finance to use this asset as collateral for a loan or as margin to open a levered derivative position. Because DeFi relies on shared interfaces, applications can directly plug into each other's assets, repackage, and subdivide positions as needed. DeFi has the potential to unlock liquidity in traditionally illiquid assets through tokenization. A simple use case would be creating fractional shares from a unitary asset such as a stock. We can extend this concept to give fractional ownership to scarce resources such as rare art.

The tokens can be used as collateral for any other DeFi service, such as leverage or derivatives.

We can invert this paradigm to create token bundles of groups of real-world or digital assets and trade them like an ETF. Imagine a dApp like a real estate investment trust (REIT), but with the added capability of allowing the owner to subdivide the REIT into the individual real estate components to select a preferred geographic distribution and allocation within the REIT. Owning the token means overseeing how the properties are distributed. The token can be traded on a decentralized exchange to liquidate the position.

Compared with digital assets, tokenizing hard assets, such as real estate or precious metals, is more difficult because the practical considerations such as maintenance and storage cannot be enforced by code. Legal restrictions across jurisdictions are also a challenge for tokenization; nevertheless, the utility of secure, contractual tokenization for most use cases should not be underestimated.

A tokenized version of a position in a DeFi platform is a pluggable derivative asset that is usable in another platform. Tokenization allows the benefits and features of one position to be portable. The archetypal example of portability through tokenization is Compound (see Chapter 6), which allows for robust lending markets in which a position – itself a token – can accrue variable-rate interest denominated in a given token. If, for example, the base asset is ETH, the ETH deposit wrapper known as cETH (cToken) can be used in place of the base asset. The result is an ETH-backed derivative that is also accruing variable-rate interest per the Compound protocol. Tokenization therefore unlocks new revenue models for dApps because they can plug asset holdings directly into Compound or use the cToken interface to gain the benefits of Compound's interest rates.

Networked Liquidity

The concept of interoperability extends easily to liquidity in the exchange use case. Traditional exchanges – in particular those that retail investors typically use – cannot readily share liquidity with other exchanges. In DeFi, as a subcomponent of the contract, any exchange application can leverage the liquidity and rates of any other exchange on the same blockchain. This capability allows for networked liquidity and leads to very competitive rates for users within the same application.

VI

DeFi DEEP DIVE

DeFi can be loosely broken into sectors based on the functionality type of the dApp. Many dApps could fit into multiple categories, so we attempt to place them into the most relevant category. We examine DeFi platforms in the taxonomy of lending/credit facilities, DEXes, derivatives, and tokenization.[1] We mainly focus on the Ethereum network due to its popularity, but DeFi innovations are occurring on many blockchains including Stellar and EOS.[2] Polkadot[3] is another platform that employs a type of proof-of-stake consensus.

CREDIT/LENDING

MakerDAO

MakerDAO[4] (DAO is a *decentralized autonomous organization*) is often considered an exemplar of DeFi. For a series of applications to build on each other, there must necessarily be a foundation. The primary value-add of MakerDAO is the creation of a cryptocollateralized stablecoin, pegged to USD. This means the system can run completely from within the Ethereum blockchain without relying on outside centralized institutions to back, vault, and audit the stablecoin. MakerDAO is a two-token model where a governance token MKR yields voting rights on the platform and participates in value capture. The second token is a stablecoin called DAI – a staple token in the DeFi ecosystem with which many protocols integrate, including a few we will discuss later.

DAI is generated as follows. A user can deposit ETH or other supported ERC-20 assets into a *vault*, which is a smart contract that escrows collateral and keeps track of the USD-denominated value of the collateral. The user can then mint DAI up to a certain collateralization ratio on their assets. This creates a "debt" in DAI that the vault holder must pay back. The DAI is the corresponding asset that can be used any way the vault holder wishes. For example, the user can sell the DAI for cash or leverage it into more of the collateral asset[5] and repeat the process. Due to the volatility of ETH and most collateral types, the collateralization requirement is far in excess of 100 percent and usually in the 150–200 percent range.

The basic idea underlying the DAI mechanism is not new; it is simply a collateralized debt position. For example, a homeowner in need of some liquidity can pledge their house as collateral to a bank and receive a mortgage loan structured to include a cash takeout. The price volatility of ETH is much greater than for a house; as such, collateralization ratios for the ETH–DAI contract are higher than a traditional mortgage. In addition, no centralized institution is necessary because everything happens within the Ethereum blockchain.

Let's consider a simple example. Suppose an ETH owner needs liquidity but does not want to sell her ETH because she thinks it will appreciate. The situation is analogous to the homeowner who needs liquidity but does not want to sell their house. Let's say an investor has 5 ETH at a market price of $200 (total value of $1,000). If the collateralization requirement is 150 percent, then the investor can mint up to 667 DAI ($1,000/1.5 with rounding). The collateralization ratio is set high to reduce the probability that the loan debt exceeds the collateral value. In addition, for the DAI token to be credibly pegged to the USD, the system needs to avoid the risk that the collateral is worth less than $1 = 1 DAI.

Given the collateralization ratio of 1.5, it would be unwise to mint the 667 DAI because if the ETH ever dropped below $200 the contract would be undercollateralized – the equivalent of a *margin call*. We are using traditional finance parlance, but in DeFi there is no communication from your broker about the need to post additional margin or to liquidate the position and also no grace period. Liquidation can happen immediately.

As such, most investors choose to mint less than 667 DAI to give themselves a buffer. Suppose the investor mints 500 DAI, which implies a collateralization ratio of 2.0 ($1,000/2.0 = 500). Let's explore two scenarios. First, suppose the price of ETH rises by 50 percent so that the collateral is worth $1,500. Now, the investor can increase the size of their loan. To maintain the collateralization of 200 percent, the investor can mint an extra 250 DAI.

A more interesting scenario is when the value of the collateral drops. Suppose the value of the ETH drops by 25 percent, from $200 to $150. In this case, the value of the collateral drops to $750 and the collateralization ratio drops to 1.5 ($750/1.5 = 500).

The vault holder faces three scenarios. First, they can increase the amount of collateral in the contract (by, e.g., adding 1 ETH). Second, they can use the 500 DAI to pay back the loan and repatriate the 5 ETH. These ETH are now worth $250 less, but the depreciation in value would have happened regardless of the loan. Third, the loan is liquidated by a *keeper* (any external actor) who is incentivized to find contracts eligible for liquidation. The keeper auctions the ETH for enough DAI to pay off the loan. In this case, 3.33 ETH would be sold and 1.47 would be returned to the vault holder (the keeper earns an incentive fee of 0.2 ETH). The vault holder then has 500 DAI worth $500 and 1.47 ETH worth $220. This analysis does not include gas fees.

Two forces in this process reinforce the stability of DAI: overcollateralization and market actions. In the liquidation, ETH are sold and DAI are purchased, which exerts positive price pressure on DAI. This simple example does not address many features in the MakerDAO ecosystem (Figure 6.1), in particular the fee mechanisms and the debt limit, which we will now explore.

DeFi Deep Dive

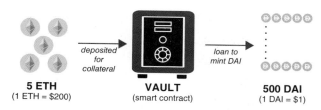

5 ETH
(1 ETH = $200)

deposited for collateral

VAULT
(smart contract)

loan to mint DAI

500 DAI
(1 DAI = $1)

VALUE of COLLATERAL (5 ETH) = $1,000

| 333 | 167 | 500 |

over collateralization   buffer   500 DAI minted

collateralization factor: **150%**
maximum loan: **1,000/1.5 = 667 DAI**
actual loan: **500 DAI**

Scenario 1   ## ETH appreciates 50% $200 —> $300

VALUE of COLLATERAL (5 ETH) = $1500

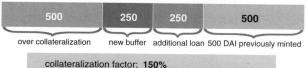

| 500 | 250 | 250 | 500 |

over collateralization   new buffer   additional loan   500 DAI previously minted

collateralization factor: **150%**
maximum loan: **1,500/1.5 = 1,000 DAI**
actual loan: **500 DAI** —> (ratio now 300%)
additional loan: **250 DAI**
new loan: **750 DAI** —> (ratio 200%)

Scenario 2   ## ETH depreciates 25% $200 —> $150

VALUE of COLLATERAL (5 ETH) = $750

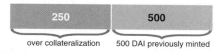

| 250 | 500 |

over collateralization   500 DAI previously minted

collateralization factor: **150%**
maximum loan: **750/1.5 = 500 DAI**
actual loan: **500 DAI** —> (ratio now 150%)

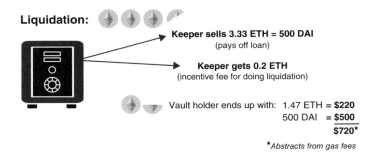

Liquidation:

Keeper sells 3.33 ETH = 500 DAI
(pays off loan)

Keeper gets 0.2 ETH
(incentive fee for doing liquidation)

Vault holder ends up with: 1.47 ETH = **$220**
500 DAI   = **$500**
   $720*

*Abstracts from gas fees

Figure 6.1   The Mechanics of MakerDAO's DAI

The viability of the MakerDAO ecosystem critically depends on DAI maintaining a 1:1 peg to the USD. Various mechanisms are in place to incentivize demand and supply to drive the price toward the peg. The primary mechanisms for maintaining the peg are the debt ceiling, stability fee, and DAI savings rate (DSR). These parameters are controlled by holders of the governance token Maker (MKR) and MakerDAO governance, which we will discuss toward the end of this section.

The stability fee is a variable interest rate that vault holders pay in DAI on any DAI debt they generate. The interest rate can be raised or lowered (even to a negative value) to incentivize the generation or repayment of DAI to drive its price toward the peg. The stability fee funds the DSR, a variable rate any DAI holder can earn on their DAI deposit. The DSR compounds on a per-block basis. The stability fee, which must always be greater or equal to the DSR, is enforced by the smart contracts powering the platform. The analogous situation in centralized finance is that the loan rate is always higher than the deposit rate. Lastly, a smart contract–enforced DAI debt ceiling can be adjusted to allow for more or less supply to meet the current level of demand. If the protocol is at the debt ceiling, no new DAI is able to be minted in new vaults until the old debt is paid or the ceiling is raised.

To stay above the liquidation threshold, a user can deposit more collateral into the vault to keep the DAI safely collateralized. When a position is deemed to be under the liquidation ratio, a keeper can initiate an auction (i.e., sell some of the ETH collateral[6]) to liquidate the position and close the vault holder's debt. The *liquidation penalty* is calculated as a percentage of the debt and is deducted from the collateral in addition to the amount needed to close the position.

After the auction, any remaining collateral reverts to the vault owner. The liquidation penalty acts as an incentive for market participants to monitor the vaults and to trigger an auction when a position becomes undercollateralized. If the collateral drops so far in value that the DAI debt cannot be fully repaid, the position is closed and the protocol accrues *protocol debt*. A buffer pool of DAI exists to cover it up to a certain amount. The solution involves the governance token MKR and the governance system.

The MKR token controls MakerDAO. Holders of the token have the right to vote on protocol upgrades, including supporting new collateral types and tweaking parameters such as collateralization ratios. MKR holders are expected to make decisions in the best financial interest of the platform.

Their incentive is that a healthy platform should increase the value of their share in the platform's governance. For example, because of poor governance, the buffer pool could be insufficient to pay back the protocol debt. If all other measures to repay the debt have failed, *global settlement* is a safety mechanism that can be used in which newly minted MKR tokens are auctioned off in exchange for DAI and the DAI are used to repay the debt. Global settlement dilutes the MKR share, so stakeholders are incentivized to avoid it and keep protocol debt to a minimum.

MKR holders are collectively the owners of the future of MakerDAO. A proposal and corresponding approved vote can change any of the parameters available on the platform. Other possible parameter changes include supporting new collateral types for vaults and adding upgrades to functionality. MKR holders could, for instance, vote to pay themselves a dividend funded by the spread between the interest payments paid by vault holders and the DAI savings rate. The reward of receiving this dividend would need to be weighed against any negative community response (e.g., a backlash against rent seeking from a previously no-rent protocol) that might decrease the value of the protocol and the MKR token.

A number of features make DAI attractive to users. Importantly, users can purchase and use DAI without having to generate it in a vault – they can simply purchase DAI on an exchange without needing to know the underlying mechanics of how they are created. Holders can easily earn the DAI savings rate by using the protocol, and more technologically and financially sophisticated users can use the MakerDAO web portal to generate vaults and create DAI to get liquidity from their assets without having to sell them. It is easy to sell DAI and purchase an additional amount of the collateral asset to get leverage.

A noteworthy drawback to DAI is that its supply is always constrained by demand for ETH-collateralized debt. No clear arbitrage loop exists to maintain the peg. For example, the stablecoin USDC is always redeemable with no fees by Coinbase for $1. Arbitrageurs have a guaranteed (assuming solvency of Coinbase) strategy in which they can buy USDC at a discount or sell it at a premium elsewhere and redeem on Coinbase. This is not true for DAI. Irrespective of any drawbacks, the simplicity of DAI makes it an essential building block for other DeFi applications (Table 6.1).

Table 6.1   The Problems That MakerDAO Solves

Traditional Finance Problem	MakerDAO Solution
Centralized control: Interest rates are influenced by the U.S. Federal Reserve and access to loan products controlled by regulation and institutional policies.	MakerDAO platform is openly controlled by the MKR holders.

(Continued)

Table 6.1   (Continued)

Traditional Finance Problem	MakerDAO Solution
Limited access: Obtaining loans is difficult for a large majority of the population.	Open ability to take out DAI liquidity against an overcollateralized position in any supported ERC-20 token. Access to a competitive USD-denominated return in the DSR.
Inefficiency: Acquiring a loan involves costs of time and money.	Instant liquidity at the push of a button with minimal transaction costs.
Lack of interoperability: Cannot trustlessly use USD or USD-collateralized token in smart contract agreements.	Issuance of DAI, a permissionless USD-tracking stablecoin backed by cryptocurrency. DAI can be used in any smart contract or DeFi application.
Opacity: Unclear collateralization of lending institutions.	Transparent collateralization ratios of vaults visible to entire ecosystem.

Compound

Compound is a lending market that offers several different ERC-20 assets for borrowing and lending. All the tokens in a single market are pooled together so every lender earns the same variable rate, and every borrower pays the same variable rate. The concept of a credit rating is irrelevant, and because Ethereum accounts are pseudonymous, enforcing repayment in the event of a loan default is virtually impossible. For this reason, all loans are overcollateralized in a collateral asset different from the one being borrowed. If a borrower fall below their collateralization ratio, their position is liquidated to pay back their debt. The debt can be liquidated by a keeper, similar to the process used in MakerDAO vaults. The keeper receives a bonus incentive for each unit of debt they close out.

The collateralization ratio is calculated via a *collateral factor*. Each ERC-20 asset on the platform has its own collateral factor ranging from 0 to 90 percent. A collateral factor of zero means an asset cannot be used as collateral. The required collateralization ratio for a single collateral type is calculated as 100 divided by the collateral factor. Volatile assets generally have lower collateral factors, which mandate higher collateralization ratios due to increased risk of a price movement that could lead to undercollateralization. An account can use multiple collateral types at once, in which case the collateralization ratio is calculated as 100 divided by the weighted average of the collateral types by their relative sizes (denominated in a common currency) in the portfolio.

The collateralization ratio is similar to a reserve multiplier in traditional banking, constraining the amount of "borrowed" dollars that can be in the system relative to the "real" supply. For instance, there is occasionally more DAI in Compound than is actually supplied by MakerDAO because users are borrowing and resupplying or selling to others who resupply. Importantly, all MakerDAO supply is ultimately backed by real collateral, and there is no way to borrow more collateral value than has been supplied.

For example, suppose an investor deposits 100 DAI with a collateral factor of 90. This transaction alone corresponds to a required collateralization ratio of 111 percent. Assuming 1 DAI = $1, the investor can borrow up to $90 worth of any other asset in Compound. If he or she borrows the maximum and the price of the borrowed asset increases at all, the position is subject to liquidation. Suppose the investor also deposit two ETH with a collateral factor of 60 and a price of $200/ETH. The total supply balance is now $500, with 80 percent being ETH and 20 percent being DAI. The required collateralization ratio is 100/(0.8*60 + 0.2*90) = 151 percent (Figure 6.2).

The supply and borrow interest rates are compounded every block (approximately 15 seconds on Ethereum producing near continuous compounding) and are determined by the utilization percentage in the market. Utilization is calculated as total borrow/total supply. The utilization rate is used as an input parameter to a formula that determines the interest rates. The remaining parameters are set by *Compound Governance,* which we describe near the end of this section.

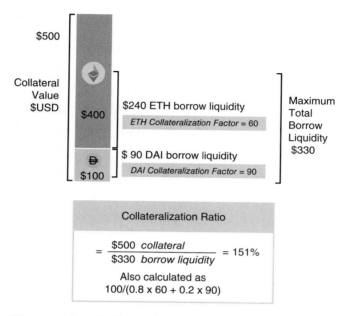

Figure 6.2   Collateralization Ratios in Compound

The formula for the borrow rate generally is an increasing linear function with a y intercept known as the *base rate* that represents the borrow rate at 0 percent borrow demand and a *slope* that represents the rate of change of the rates. These parameters are different for each ERC-20 asset supported by the platforms. Some markets have more advanced formulas that include a *kink*, which is a utilization ratio beyond which the slope steepens. These formulas can be used to reduce the cost of borrowing up to the kink and then increase the cost of borrowing after the kink to incentivize a minimum level of liquidity.

The supply interest rate is the borrow rate multiplied by the utilization ratio so that borrow payments can fully cover the supplier rates. The *reserve factor* is a percentage of the borrow payments not given to the suppliers and instead set aside in a reserve pool that acts as insurance in case a borrower defaults. In an extreme price movement, many positions may become undercollateralized in that they have insufficient funds to repay the suppliers. In the event of such a scenario, the suppliers would be repaid using the assets in the reserve pool.

Here is a concrete example of the rate mechanics. In the DAI market, 100 million DAI is supplied, and 50 million is borrowed. Suppose the base rate is 1 percent and the slope is 10 percent. At 50 million borrowed, utilization is 50 percent. The borrow interest rate is then calculated to be $0.5*0.1 + 0.01 = 0.06$, or 6 percent. The maximum supply rate (assuming a reserve factor of zero) would simply be $0.5*0.06 = 0.03$, or 3 percent. If the reserve factor is set to 10, then 10 percent of the borrow interest is diverted to a DAI reserve pool, lowering the supply interest rate to 2.7 percent. Another way to think about the supply interest rate is that the 6 percent borrow interest of 50 million is equal to 3 million of borrow payments. Distributing 3 million of payments to 100 million of suppliers implies a 3 percent interest rate to all suppliers.

For a more complicated example involving a kink, suppose 100 million DAI is supplied, and 90 million DAI is borrowed – a 90 percent utilization. The kink is at 80 percent utilization, before which the slope is 10 percent and after which the slope is 40 percent, which implies the borrow rate will be much higher if the 80 percent utilization is exceeded.

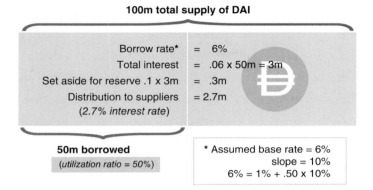

100m total supply of DAI

Borrow rate* = 6%
Total interest = .06 x 50m = 3m
Set aside for reserve .1 x 3m = .3m
Distribution to suppliers = 2.7m
(2.7% interest rate)

50m borrowed
(utilization ratio = 50%)

* Assumed base rate = 6%
slope = 10%
6% = 1% + .50 x 10%

Figure 6.3   Savings and Lending Rates in Compound

The base rate remains at 1 percent. The borrow interest rate = 0.01 (base) + 0.8*0.1 (pre-kink) + 0.1*0.4 (post-kink) = 13 percent. The supply rate (assuming a reserve factor of zero) is 0.9*0.13 = 11.7 percent (Figure 6.3).

The utility of the Compound lending market is straight-forward: it allows users to unlock the value of an asset without selling it and incurring a taxable event (at least under today's rules), similar to a home equity line of credit. Additionally, they can use the borrowed assets to engineer leveraged long or short positions, with competitive pooled rates and no approval process. For instance, if an investor is bearish on the price of ETH, they can simply deposit a stablecoin, such as DAI or USDC, as collateral and then borrow ETH and sell it for more of the stablecoin. If the price of ETH falls, investors use some of the DAI to purchase (cheaply) ETH to repay the debt. Compound offers several volatile and stable tokens to suit the risk preferences of investors, and new tokens are continually added.

The Compound protocol must escrow tokens as a depositor to maintain that liquidity for the platform itself and to keep track of each person's ownership stake in each market. It would be naïve to keep track of the number inside a contract; instead, it would be better to tokenize the user's share. Compound does this using a cToken, one of the platform's important innovations.

Compound's cToken is an ERC-20 in its own right and represents an ownership stake in the underlying Compound market. For example, cDAI corresponds to the Compound DAI market, and cETH corresponds to the Compound ETH market. Both tokens are minted and burned in proportion to the funds added and removed from the underlying market as a means to track the amount belonging to a specific investor. Because of the interest payments that continually accrue to suppliers, these tokens are always worth more than the underlying asset. The benefit of designing the protocol in this way is that a cToken can be traded on its own like a normal ERC-20 asset. This trait allows other protocols to seamlessly integrate with Compound simply by holding cTokens and allows users to deploy their cTokens directly into other opportunities, such as using a cToken as collateral for a MakerDAO vault. Instead of using ETH only as collateral, an investors can use cETH and earn lending interest on the ETH collateral.

For example, assume there are 2,000 DAI in the Compound DAI market, and a total 500 cDAI represents the ownership in the market; this ratio of cDAI to DAI is not determinative and could just as easily be 500,000 cDAI. At that moment in the example, 1 cDAI is worth 4 DAI, but after more interest accrues in the market the ratio will change. If a trader comes in and deposits 1,000 DAI, the supply increases by 50 percent (Figure 6.4). Therefore, the Compound protocol mints 50 percent more cDAI (250 cDAI) and transfers this amount to the trader's account. Assuming an interest rate of 10 percent, at year end there will be 3,300 DAI, and the trader's 250 cDAI can be redeemed for one-third, or 1,100,

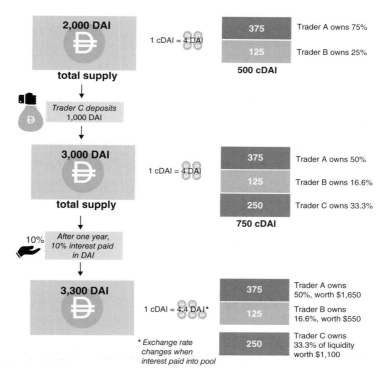

Figure 6.4 The Mechanics of Compound's Equity Token (cToken)

of the DAI. The trader can deploy cDAI in the place of DAI so that the DAI is not sitting idle but earning interest via the Compound pool. For example, the trader could deploy cDAI as the necessary collateral to open a perpetual futures position on dYdX or she could market make on Uniswap using a cDAI trading pair. (dYdX and Uniswap are discussed later in the chapter.)

The many different parameters of Compound's functionality – such as the *collateral factor, reserve factor, base rate, slope,* and *kink* – can all be tuned. The entity capable of tuning these parameters is Compound Governance, which has the power to change parameters, add new markets, freeze the ability to initiate new deposits or borrows in a market, and even upgrade some of the contract code itself. Importantly, Compound Governance cannot steal funds or prevent users from withdrawing. In the early stages of Compound's growth, governance was controlled by developer admins, similar to any tech startup. A strong development goal of Compound, as with most DeFi protocols, was to remove developer admin access and release the protocol to the leadership of a DAO via a governance token. The token allowed shareholders and community members to collectively become Compound Governance and propose upgrades or parameter tuning. A quorum agreement was required for any change to be implemented.[7]

Compound implemented this new governance system in May 2020 via the COMP token. COMP is used to vote on protocol updates such as parameter tuning, addition of new asset support, and functionality upgrades (similar to MKR for MakerDAO). On June 15, 2020, the seventh governance proposal passed, which provided for distributing COMP tokens to users of the platform based on the borrow volume per market.[8] The proposal offered an experience akin to a tech company giving its own stock to its users. The COMP token is distributed to both suppliers and borrowers and acts as a subsidization of rates. With the release of the token on public markets, COMP's market cap spiked to over $2 billion. The price point of the distribution rate is so high that borrowing in most markets turned out to be profitable. This arbitrage opportunity attracted considerable volume to the platform, and the community governance has made and passed several proposals to help manage the usage.

The Compound protocol can no longer be turned off and will remain on Ethereum as long as Ethereum exists. Other platforms can easily escrow funds in Compound to provide additional value to their users or enable novel business models. An interesting example of this is Pool-Together,[9] a no-loss lottery[10] that deposits all user's funds into Compound but pays the entire pool's earned interest to a single random depositor at fixed intervals. Easy, instant access to yield or borrow liquidity on different Ethereum tokens makes Compound an important platform in DeFi (Table 6.2).

Table 6.2   Problems That Compound Solves

Traditional Finance Problem	Compound Solution
Centralized control: Borrowing and lending rates are controlled by institutions.	Compound rates are determined algorithmically and give control of market parameters to COMP stakeholders incentivized to provide value to users.
Limited access: Difficulty in accessing high-yield USD investment opportunities or competitive borrowing.	Open ability to borrow or lend any supported assets at competitive algorithmically determined rates (temporarily subsidized by COMP distribution).
Inefficiency: Suboptimal rates for borrowing and lending due to inflated costs.	Algorithmically pooled and optimized interest rates.
Lack of interoperability: Cannot repurpose supplied positions for other investment opportunities.	Tokenized positions via cTokens can be used to turn static assets into yield-generating assets.
Opacity: Unclear collateralization of lending institutions.	Transparent collateralization ratios of borrowers visible to entire ecosystem.

Aave

Aave[11] (launched in 2017) is a lending market protocol similar to Compound and offers several enhanced features. Aave offers many additional tokens to supply and borrow beyond what Compound offers. At the time of writing, Compound offers nine distinct tokens (different ERC-20 Ethereum-based assets), and Aave offers these nine plus an additional 13 not offered on Compound. Importantly, the Aave lending and variable borrowing rates are more predictable because, unlike the volatile COMP token in Compound, no subsidy is involved.

The Aave protocol supports the ability to create entirely new markets. Each market consists of its own group of token pools with their corresponding supply and borrow interest rates. The benefit of creating a separate market is that the market's supported tokens act as collateral solely in that market and cannot affect other markets, thus mitigating any potential contagion.

Aave currently has two main markets. The first is for more conventional ERC-20 tokens similar to those of Compound, supporting assets such as ETH, USDC, and DAI. The second is specific to Uniswap LP tokens. For example, when a user deposits collateral into a Uniswap market (known as a liquidity pool), they receive an LP token that represents their ownership in the market. The LP tokens can be deposited in the Uniswap market on Aave to generate additional returns.

Aave also supports flash loans in all of its markets and is the only source of flash liquidity for many smaller-cap tokens. Aave charges a fee of 9 basis points (bps) on the loan amount to execute a flash loan. The fee is paid to the asset pool and provides an additional return on investment to suppliers because they each own a pro rata share of the pool. An important use case for flash loans is that they allow users quick access to capital as a means to refinance positions. This functionality is crucial to DeFi, both as general infrastructure and as a component of a positive user experience (UX).

To provide an example, assume the price of ETH is 200 DAI. A user supplies 100 ETH in Compound and borrows 10,000 DAI to lever up and purchase an additional 50 ETH, which the user also supplies to Compound. Suppose the borrow interest rate in DAI on Compound is 15 percent, but only Aave is 5 percent. The goal is to refinance the borrowing to take advantage of the lower rate offered on Aave, which is analogous to refinancing a mortgage, a long and costly process in centralized finance.

One option is to manually unwind each trade on Compound and redo both trades on Aave to reconstruct the levered position, but this option is wasteful in terms of exchange fees and gas fees. The easier route is to take out a flash loan from Aave for 10,000 DAI, use it to pay the debt on Compound, withdraw the full 150 ETH, resupply to Aave, and trigger a normal Aave borrow position (at 5 percent APR) against that collateral to repay the flash loan (Figure 6.5). The latter approach effectively skips the

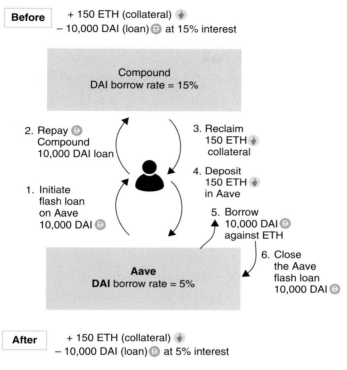

Figure 6.5   The Mechanics of an Aave Flash Loan

steps of exchanging ETH for DAI to unwind and rewind the leverage.

As shown in the preceding example, a flash loan used to refinance a position allows for DeFi client applications that let users migrate a levered position from one dApp to another with the single push of a button. These applications can even optimize portfolios for APR among several competing offerings, including Maker DSR (Dai Savings Rate), Compound, dYdX, and Aave.

An Aave innovation (and as of this writing available only on Aave) is a stable rate loan. (Using the label *stable* intentionally avoids calling it *fixed rate*.) A borrower has the option to switch between the variable rate and the current stable rate. The supply rate is always variable because under certain circumstances, such as if all borrowers left the market, it would be impossible to fund a fixed supply rate. The suppliers always collectively earn the sum of the stable and variable borrow interest payments minus any fees to the platform.

The stable rate is not a fixed rate because the rate is adjustable in extreme liquidity crunches and can be refinanced to a lower rate if market conditions allow. Also, some constraints exist around how much liquidity can be removed at a specific stable rate. Algorithmic stable borrowing rates provide value to risk-averse investors who wish to take on leverage without the uncertainty of a variable-rate position.

Aave is developing a *credit delegation* feature in which users can allocate collateral to potential borrowers who can use it to borrow a desired asset. Unsecured and reliant on trust, this process allows for uncollateralized loan relationships, such as in traditional finance, and potentially opens the floodgates in terms of sourcing liquidity. The credit delegation agreements will likely have fees and credit scores to compensate for the risk of unsecured loans. Ultimately, the delegator has sole discretion to determine who is an eligible borrower and what contract terms are sufficient. Importantly, credit delegation terms can be mediated by a smart contract. Alternatively, the delegated liquidity can be given to a smart contract that can use the liquidity to accomplish its intended function. The underlying benefit of credit delegation is that all loans in Aave are ultimately backed by collateral, regardless of whose collateral it is.

For example, a supplier may have a balance of 40,000 DAI in Aave earning interest. The supplier wants to increase their expected return via an unsecured delegation of their collateral to a trusted counterparty. The supplier likely knows the counterparty through an off-chain relationship – perhaps a banking client. The counterparty can proceed to borrow, for instance, 100 ETH with the commitment to repay the asset to the supplier plus an agreed on interest payment. The practical impact is that the external relationship is unsecured because no collateral is available to enforce payment; the relationship is based essentially on trust.

In summary, Aave offers several innovations beyond the lending products offered by Compound and other competitors. Aave's flash loans, although not unique among competitors, provide additional yield to investors, making them a compelling mechanism to provide liquidity. These utilities also attract to the platform arbitrageurs and other applications that require flash liquidity for their use cases. Stable borrow rates are a key innovation, and Aave is the only platform currently with this offering. This feature could be important for larger players who cannot operate under the potential volatility of variable borrow rates.

Finally, credit delegation allows users to unlock the value of supplied collateral in novel ways, including through traditional markets and contracts and even via additional layers of smart contracts that charge a premium rate to compensate for risk. Credit delegation allows loan providers to take their own collateral in the form of non-fungible Ethereum assets, perhaps tokenized art or real estate not supported by the main Aave protocol. As Aave continues to innovate, the platform will continue to amass more liquidity and cover a wider base of potential use cases (Table 6.3).

Table 6.3   Problems That Aave Solves

Traditional Finance Problem	Aave Solution
Centralized control: Borrowing and lending rates controlled by institutions.	Aave interest rates are controlled algorithmically.
Limited access: Only select groups have access to large quantities of money for arbitrage or refinancing.	Flash loans democratize access to liquid immediately profitable enterprises.
Inefficiency: Suboptimal rates for borrowing and lending due to inflated costs.	Algorithmically pooled and optimized interest rates.

(Continued)

Table 6.3   (Continued)

Traditional Finance Problem	Aave Solution
Lack of interoperability: Cannot monetize or utilize excess collateral in a lending position.	Credit delegation allows parties to use deposited collateral when they do not need borrowing liquidity.
Opacity: Unclear collateralization of lending institutions.	Transparent collateralization ratios of borrowers visible to the entire ecosystem.

DECENTRALIZED EXCHANGE

Uniswap

The primary example of an AMM on Ethereum is Uniswap.[12] We will focus our discussion on Uniswap v2. Recently, the third iteration of Uniswap was released and the v3 will be discussed later. Uniswap v2 uses a constant product rule to determine the trading price, using the formula $k = x^*y$, where x is the balance of asset A, and y the balance of asset B. The product k is the *invariant* and is required to remain fixed at a given level of liquidity. To purchase (withdraw) some x, some y must be sold (deposited). The implied price is x/y and is the *risk-neutral* price because the contract is equally willing to buy or sell at this rate as long as invariant *k* is constant.

Consider a concrete example (Figure 6.6). For simplicity, we will ignore transaction fees (gas) in all of the examples. Assume an investor in the Uniswap USDC/DAI market has 4 DAI (Asset A) and 4 USDC (Asset B). This sets the instantaneous exchange rate at 1 DAI:1 USDC and the invariant at 16 ($= x^*y$). To sell 4 DAI for USDC, the investor deposits 4 DAI to the contract and withdraws 2 USDC. Now the USDC balance is $4 - 2 = 2$ and the DAI balance is $4 + 4 = 8$. The invariant remains constant at 16. Notice that the effective exchange rate is now 2 DAI: 1 USDC. The change in the exchange rate is due to slippage because of the low level of liquidity in the market. The magnitude of the invariant determines the amount of slippage. To extend the example, assume the balance is 100 DAI and 100 USDC in the contract. Now the invariant is 10,000, but the exchange rate is the same. If the investor sells 4 DAI for USDC, now 3.85 USDC can be withdrawn to keep the invariant constant and results in much lower slippage at an effective rate of 1.04 DAI: 1 USDC.

Deep liquidity helps minimize slippage. Therefore, it is important that Uniswap incentivizes depositors to supply capital to a given market. Anyone can become a liquidity provider by supplying assets on both sides of a market at the current exchange rate.[13] Supplying both sides increases the product of the amount of assets held in the trading pair (i.e., increases the invariant as mentioned in the formula for

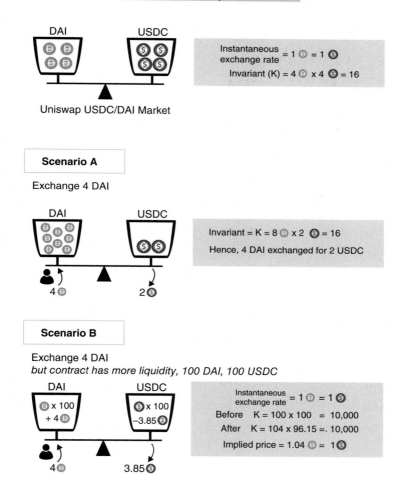

Figure 6.6   The Mechanics of a Uniswap Automated Market Maker

the market maker). Following the preceding example, higher invariants lead to lower slippage and therefore an increase in effective liquidity. We can think of the invariant as a direct measure of liquidity. In summary, liquidity providing increases the invariant with no effect on price, whereas trading against a market impacts the price with no effect on the invariant.

Each trade in a Uniswap market has an associated 0.3 percent fee that is paid back into the pool. Liquidity providers earn these fees based on their pro rata contribution to the liquidity pool and therefore prefer high-volume markets. This mechanism of earning fees is identical to the *cToken* model of Compound. The ownership stake is represented by a similar token called a UNI token. For example, the token representing ownership in the DAI/ETH pool is UNI DAI/ETH.

Liquidity providers in Uniswap essentially earn passive income in proportion to the volume on the market they are supplying. On withdrawal, however, the exchange rate of the underlying assets will almost certainly have changed. This shift creates an opportunity–cost dynamic (*impermanent loss*) that arises because the liquidity provider could simply hold the underlying assets and profit from the price movement. The fees earned from trading volume must exceed impermanent loss for liquidity providing to be profitable. Consequently, stablecoin trading pairs such as USDC/DAI are attractive for liquidity providers because the high correlation of the assets minimizes the impermanent loss.

Uniswap's $k = x^*y$ pricing model works well if the correlation of the underlying assets is unknown. The model calculates the exact same slippage at a given liquidity level for any two trading pairs. In practice, however, we would expect much lower slippage for a stablecoin trading pair than for an ETH trading pair because we know by design that the stablecoin's price should be close to $1. The Uniswap pricing model leaves money on the table for arbitrageurs on high correlation pairs such as stablecoins because it does not adjust default slippage lower (change the shape of the bonding curve) as expected; the profit is subtracted from the liquidity providers. For this reason, competitor AMMs such as Curve[14] that specialize in high-correlation trading pairs may cannibalize liquidity in these types of Uniswap markets.

If the pair does not already exist, anyone can start an ERC-20/ERC-20 or ETH/ERC-20 trading pair on Uniswap by simply supplying capital on both sides.[15] The user determines the initial exchange rate, and arbitrageurs should drive that price to the true market price if it deviates at all. Users of the platform can effectively trade any two ERC-20 tokens supported by using *router contracts* that determine the most efficient path of swaps to get the lowest slippage if no direct trading pair is available.

A drawback of the AMM model is that it is particularly susceptible to front-running. This is not to be confused with illegal front-running, which plagues centralized finance. One of the features of blockchain is that all transactions are public. That is, when an Ethereum user posts a transaction to the memory pool, it is publicly visible to all Ethereum nodes. Front-runners can see this transaction – which is public information – and post a higher gas fee to trade against the pair before the user's transaction is added to a block; then they can immediately trade in the reverse direction against the pair. Estimates of front-running revenues, which come directly at the expense of the users, grew from hundreds of thousands of dollars when front-running was first publicly demonstrated in 2017,[16] to hundreds of millions of dollars as of mid-2021.[17] Large transactions, especially in illiquid markets with high slippage, are particularly susceptible to front-running. For this reason, Uniswap allows users to set a maximum slippage as a clause in the transaction. If the acceptable level of slippage is exceeded, the trade will fail to execute.[18] This provides a limit to the profit front-runners can make but does not completely remove the problem.

Another drawback is that arbitrage profits go only to arbitrageurs – they do not have a vested interest in the platform. The arbitrageurs profit at the expense of liquidity providers, who should not be losing the potential spread they would earn in a normal market-making scenario. Competing platforms, such as Mooniswap,[19] propose to solve this issue by supplying virtual prices that slowly approach the true price, leaving tighter time windows and lower spreads for arbitrageurs to capitalize on. The additional spread remains in the pool for the liquidity providers.

Uniswap offers an interesting feature called a *flash swap*, which is similar to a flash loan. In a flash swap, the contract sends the tokens *before* the user pays for them with assets on the other side of the pair, unlocking many opportunities for arbitrageurs. The user can deploy this instant liquidity to acquire the other asset at a discount on another exchange before repaying it; the corresponding amount of the alternate asset must be repaid to maintain the invariant. This flexibility in a flash swap is different from the provision in a flash loan, which requires that repayment occur with the same asset. A key aspect of a flash swap is that all trades must occur during a single Ethereum transaction and the trade must be closed with the corresponding amount of the complementary asset in that market.

Consider this example in the DAI/USDC market with a supply of 100,000 each (Figure 6.7). This implies a 1:1 exchange rate and an invariant of 10 billion. A trader who

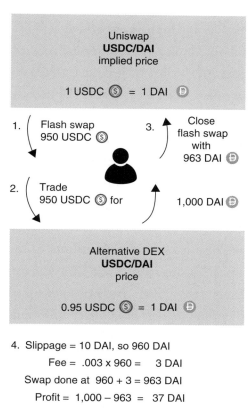

4. Slippage = 10 DAI, so 960 DAI

Fee = .003 x 960 =   3 DAI

Swap done at 960 + 3 = 963 DAI

Profit = 1,000 − 963 = 37 DAI

Figure 6.7   The Mechanics of a Flash Swap in Uniswap

has no starting capital spots an arbitrage opportunity to buy DAI on a DEX for 0.95 USDC. The trader can capitalize on this arbitrage via a flash swap by withdrawing 950 USDC of flash liquidity (liquidity derived from a flash loan) from the DAI/USDC market, purchase 1,000 DAI via the described arbitrage trade, and repay 963 DAI for a profit of 37 DAI – all consummated with no initial capital. The figure of 963 is calculated as 960 (with rounding for ease of illustration) to maintain the 10 billion invariant and to account for some slippage, plus a 0.30 percent*960 = 3 DAI transaction fee paid into the pool owned by the liquidity providers.

An important point about Uniswap is the release of a governance token in September 2020 called UNI. Like COMP, the Compound governance token, UNI is distributed to users to incentivize liquidity in key pools including ETH/USDC and ETH/DAI. The UNI governance even has some control over its own token distribution because 43 percent of the supply will be vested over four years to a treasury controlled by UNI governance. Importantly, each unique Ethereum address that had used Uniswap before a certain cutoff date (over 250,000 addresses) was given 400 UNI tokens as a free airdrop. At the same time as the airdrop, UNI was released on Uniswap and the Coinbase Pro exchange for trading. The price per token opened around $3 with a total market cap of over $500 million, amounting to $1,200 of liquid value distributed directly to each user. This flood of supply could have led to selling pressure that tanked the token price. Instead, the token price spiked to over $8 before settling in the $4–5 range. Through UNI, Uniswap effectively crowdsourced capital to build and scale its business, which attained a unicorn valuation for a short time. This demonstrates the value the community places in the token and the platform because the majority of supply is still held by those who received the airdrop.

As evidence that Uniswap is a good idea, it has been largely copied by Sushiswap.[20] Furthermore, the CFMM has been generalized by Balancer,[21] in which more than two markets can be supported in a liquidity pool. In addition, the assets can be arbitrarily weighted (currently, Uniswap requires equal value).[22] Further, the liquidity pool creator sets the transactions fees.

As of March 2021, the Uniswap team released a timeline and upgrade plan for the Uniswap protocol. Termed Uniswap v3, the Uniswap team proposed several changes to the protocol's liquidity provisioning model, moving away from the constant product formula described earlier and toward a model that resembles an on-chain, limit order book.[23] This change increases Uniswap's flexibility, allowing users and liquidity providers to customize curves and more actively manage their liquidity positions/control their return profiles. Uniswap v3 was launched May 5, 2021 and, as of writing, the volume of trading on v3 has already exceeded the v2 volume.[24]

Uniswap is critical infrastructure for DeFi applications; it is important to have exchanges operational whenever it is needed. Uniswap offers a unique approach for generating yield on users' assets by being a liquidity provider. The platform's flash swap functionality aids arbitrageurs in maintaining efficient markets and unlocks new use cases for users, who can access any ERC-20 token listed, including creating completely new tokens through an IDO. As AMM volume grows on Ethereum and new platforms arise with competing models, Uniswap will continue to be a leader and an example of critical infrastructure going forward (Table 6.4).

Table 6.4   Problems That Uniswap Solves

Traditional Finance Problem	Uniswap Solution
Centralized control: Exchanges that control which trading pairs are supported.	Allows anyone to create a new trading pair if it does not already exist and automatically routes trades through the most efficient path if no direct pair exists.
Limited access: The best investment opportunities and returns from liquidity providing are restricted to large institutions.	Anyone can become a liquidity provider and earn fees for doing so. Any project can list its token on Uniswap to give anyone access to an investor.
Inefficiency: Trades generally require two parties to clear.	An AMM that allows constant access for trading against the contract.

(Continued)

Table 6.4   (Continued)

Traditional Finance Problem	Uniswap Solution
Lack of interoperability: Ability to exchange assets on one exchange is not easily used within another financial application.	Any token swap needed for a DeFi application can utilize Uniswap as an embedded feature.
Opacity: Unknown if the exchange truly owns all user's entire balance.	Transparent liquidity levels in the platform and algorithmic pricing.

DERIVATIVES

Yield Protocol

Yield Protocol[25] proposes a derivative model for secured, zero-coupon bonds. Essentially, the protocol defines a *yToken* to be an ERC-20 (fungible) token that settles in some fixed quantity of a target asset at a specified date. The contract will specify that the tokens – which have the same expiry, target asset, collateral asset, and collateralization ratio – are fungible. They are secured by the collateral asset and have a required maintenance collateralization ratio similar to, for example, MakerDAO, and to other DeFi platforms we have already discussed. If the collateral's value dips below the maintenance requirement, the position can be liquidated with some or all of the collateral sold to cover the debt.

The mechanism for yToken settlement is still undecided, but one proposed solution is "cash" settlement, which means paying an equivalent amount of the collateral asset worth the specified amount of the target asset. For example, if the target asset is 1 ETH secured by 300 DAI, and at expiry 1 ETH = 200 DAI, a cash settlement would pay out 200 DAI and return the 100 DAI excess collateral to the seller of the yToken. The other commonly proposed solution is "physical" settlement, which automatically sells collateral for the target asset upon expiry (perhaps on Uniswap) to pay out in the target asset. Using the same numbers as in the previous example, the owner of the yToken would receive 1 ETH and the seller would receive slightly less of the remaining collateral, likely around 95 DAI, after subtracting exchange fees. The yToken effectively allows for fixed-rate borrowing and lending, using the implied return on the discounted price of the token versus the target amount.

We can illustrate as follows: assume a user has a yToken with the target asset of 1 DAI backed by ETH. The maturity date is one year ahead, and the yToken is trading at 0.92 DAI. A purchase of the yToken effectively secures an 8.7 percent fixed interest rate, even in the case of a liquidation. In the event of a normal liquidation, the collateral would be sold to cover the position, as shown in Figure 6.8.

A compelling third option for settlement (in addition to cash and physical) is "synthetic" settlement. Here, the

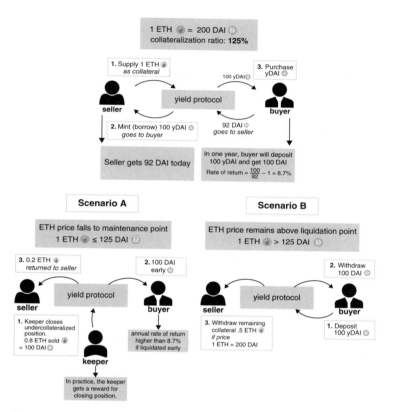

Figure 6.8   The Mechanics of Fixed-Rate Borrowing in the Yield Protocol

underlying asset is not directly repaid but instead is rolled into an equivalent amount of that asset pool on a lending platform such as Compound. Synthetic settlement means that yDAI could settle in cDAI, converting the fixed rate into a floating rate. Buyer could close the position and redeem cDAI for DAI at their leisure. The Yield Protocol handles all these conversions for users so that user experience simply revolves around the target asset.

In the Yield Protocol white paper,[26] the authors discuss interesting applications from the investor's perspective. An investor can purchase yTokens to synthetically lend the target asset. The investor would be paying X amount of the asset now to purchase the yTokens. Upon settlement, the investor receives X + interest. This financial transaction in total is functionally a lend of the target asset. Note that the interest is implied in the pricing and not a directly specified value. Alternatively, yTokens can be minted and sold to synthetically borrow the target asset, meaning X amount of the asset is received now (the face value) with the promise to pay X + interest in the future. This financial transaction is functionally a borrow of the target asset.

Additional applications include a perpetual product on top of yTokens that maintains a portfolio of different maturities and rolls short-term profits into long-term yToken contracts. For example, the portfolio may include three-, six-, and nine-month plus one-year maturity yTokens; once the three-month tokens mature, the smart contract can reinvest the balance into one-year maturity yTokens. Token holders in this fund would essentially be experiencing a floating rate yield on the underlying asset with rate updates every three months. The yTokens also allow for the construction of yield curves by analyzing the implied yields of short and longer term contracts. This allows observers to quantify investor sentiment among the various supported target assets.

The Yield Protocol can even be directly used to speculate on interest rates. Several DAI derivative assets – Compound cDAI, Aave aDAI, and Chai[25] – represent a variable interest rate. One can imagine a seller of yDAI using one of these DAI derivative assets as collateral. The effect of this transaction is that the seller is paying the fixed rate on the yDAI while receiving the variable rate on the collateral. This is a bet that rates will increase. Likewise, purchasing yDAI (of any collateral type) is a bet that variable rates will not increase beyond the fixed rate received.

Yield is an important protocol that supplies fixed rate products to Ethereum. It can be tightly integrated with other protocols like MakerDAO and Compound to create robust interest-bearing applications for investors. Demand for fixed income components will grow as mainstream investors begin adopting DeFi with portfolios in need of these types of assets (Table 6.5).

Table 6.5   Problems That the Yield Protocol Solves

Traditional Finance Problem	Yield Solution
Centralized control: Fixed income instruments largely restricted to governments and large corporations.	Yield protocol is open to parties of any size.

(Continued)

Table 6.5 (Continued)

Traditional Finance Problem	Yield Solution
Limited access: Many investors have limited access to buy or sell sophisticated fixed income investments.	Yield allows all market participants to buy or sell a fixed income asset that settles in a target asset of their choosing.
Inefficiency: Fixed income rates are lower due to layers of fat in traditional finance.	Lean infrastructure running on Ethereum allows for more competitive rates and diverse liquidity pools due to the elimination of middlemen.
Lack of interoperability: Fixed income instruments generally settle in cash that the investor must determine how to allocate.	yTokens can settle in any Ethereum target asset and even settle synthetically into a floating-rate lending protocol to preserve returns.
Opacity: Risk and uncertainty of counterparty in traditional agreements.	Clear collateralization publicly known on Ethereum blockchain backing the investment.

dYdX

dYdX[26] specializes in derivatives and margin trading, which currently supports a variety of cryptocurrencies in addition to ETH and BTC. The company has a spot DEX that allows investors to exchange these assets against the current bid–ask on the order book and uses a hybrid on–off chain approach. Essentially, dYdX stores *signed,* or preapproved, orders without submitting to Ethereum; they use cryptography to guarantee they are used only to exchange funds for the desired asset at the desired price. The DEX supports limit orders and a *maximum slippage* parameter for market orders in an effort to mitigate the slippage associated with price moves or front-running.

dYdX provides market makers and traders the open-source software and a user interface required to interact with the DEX. Having dYdX do the order matching introduces a certain element of trust because the infrastructure could be in downtime or not posting transactions for some reason. Allowing dYdX to match the orders holds little or no risk that the company could steal user funds because the signed orders can be used only as intended per the smart contract. When the orders are matched, they are submitted to the Ethereum blockchain, where the smart contract facilitates settlement.

In addition, an investor can take a levered long or short position up to 10 times using margined collateral. The positions can be isolated so that a single collateral deposit is used or cross-margined to pool investor's balances for collateral. As in other protocols, dYdX has a maintenance margin requirement that, if not maintained, triggers liquidation of the collateral to close the position. The liquidations can be performed by external keepers who are paid to find and liquidate underwater positions, similar to the process followed by MakerDAO.

dYdX offers borrowing and lending similar to Compound and Aave. It also features free flash loans (Aave's are not free), which makes it a popular choice for DAI, ETH, and USDC flash liquidity. In the world of open smart contracts, it makes sense that flash loans rates would be driven to zero since they are nearly risk-free. Lending rates are determined by the loan's duration and relative risk of default. For flash loans, repayment is algorithmically enforced, and time is infinitesimal. In a single transaction, only the user can make any function calls or transfers; no other Ethereum users can move funds or make any changes while a particular user's transaction is in flight, resulting in no opportunity cost for the capital. Hence, as expected, a market participant offering free flash loans will attract more usage to their platform. Because flash loans do not require any up-front capital, they democratize access to funds for various use cases. In the Aave example, we show how flash loans can be used to refinance a loan. We will now illustrate the use of flash loans to capitalize on an arbitrage opportunity.

Suppose the effective exchange rate for 1,000 DAI for ETH on Uniswap is 6 ETH/1,000 DAI. (The instantaneous exchange rate would be different due to slippage.) Also, suppose the dYdX DEX has a spot ask price of 5 ETH for 1,000 DAI (i.e., the ETH are much more expensive on dYdX than Uniswap). To capitalize on this arbitrage opportunity, without any capital beyond the gas fee, an investor can execute a flash loan to borrow 1,000 DAI, exchange it on Uniswap for 6 ETH, and use 5 of those ETH to trade for 1,000 DAI on dYdX. Finally, the investor can repay the flash loan with the 1,000 DAI and pocket the 1 ETH profit. This all happens in a single transaction; multiple contract executions can happen in a single transaction on the Ethereum blockchain (Figure 6.9).

The main derivative products dYdX offers are ETH and BTC perpetual futures. At the time of writing, dYdX also

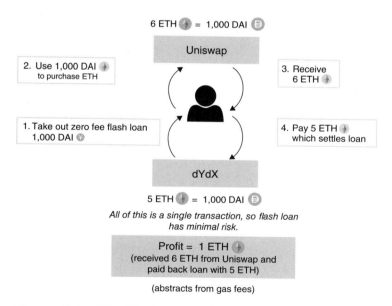

Figure 6.9   The Mechanics of Arbitrage with dYdX

offered 11 other cryptocurrency futures. A perpetual futures contract is similar to a traditional futures contract but without and expiration date. By entering into a perpetual futures contract, the investor is simply betting on the future price of an asset. The contract can be long or short and with or without leverage; it uses an index price based on the average price of the underlying asset across the major exchanges.[27] The investor deposits margin collateral and chooses a direction and amount of leverage. Depending on investor demand, the contract can trade at a premium or discount to the index price (BTC).

A funding rate, paid from one side to the other, keeps the futures price close to the index. If the futures contract is trading at a premium to the index, the funding rate would be positive and longs would pay shorts. The magnitude of the funding rate is a function of the difference in price compared with the index. Likewise, if the contract is trading at a discount, the shorts pay the long positions. The funding rate incentivizes investors to take up the opposing side from the majority to keep the contract price close to the index.[28] As long as the required margin is maintained, the investor can always close the position at the difference in the price of the notional position minus any negative balance held on margin.

Like a traditional futures contract, the perpetual futures contract has two margins: initial and maintenance. Suppose the initial margin is 10 percent. This means the investor needs to post collateral (or equity) worth 10 percent of the underlying asset. A long futures contract allows the investor to buy the asset at a set price in the future. If the market price rises, the investor can buy the asset at a price cheaper than the market price and the profit is the difference between the market price and the contract price. A short position works similarly except that the investor agrees to sell the asset at a fixed price. If the market price falls, the investor can purchase the asset in the open market and sell at the higher price stipulated in the contract. The profit is the difference between the contract price and the market price.

The risk is that the price moves against the investor. For example, if the investor is long with a 10 percent margin and the market price drops by 10 percent, the collateral is gone because the difference between purchasing at the contract price and selling in the open market (at a loss) wipes out the value of the collateral. Importantly, futures are different from options. If the underlying asset's price moves the wrong way in an option contract, the option holder can walk away: the exercise of the option is discretionary – that is why it is called an option – and no trader would exercise an option to guarantee a loss. Futures, however, are obligations. As such, traditional exchanges have mechanisms that seek to minimize the chance the contract holder does not default on a losing position.

The maintenance margin is the main tool to minimize default. Suppose the maintenance margin is 5 percent.

On a traditional futures exchange, if the price drops by 5 percent investors are required to replenish the collateral to bring it back up to 10 percent. If investors fail to do this, the exchange liquidates the position. A similar mechanism exists on dYdX, but with important differences. First, if any position falls to 5 percent, keepers will trigger liquidation. If any collateral remains, they may keep it as a reward. Second, the liquidation is almost instantaneous. Third, no centralized exchange exists. Fourth, dYdX contracts are perpetual, whereas traditional exchange contracts usually have a fixed maturity date.[29]

Consider the following example. Suppose the BTC price index is 10,000 USDC/BTC. An investor initiates a long position by depositing 1,000 USDC as margin (collateral), creating a levered bet on the price of BTC. If the price rises by 5 percent, the profit is 500. Given the investor has only deposited 1,000, the investor's rate of return is 50 percent, or (1,000 – 500)/1,000.

We can also think about the mechanics another way. Taking a long position at 10,000, the investor is committing to buying at 10,000 and the obligation is 10,000. Think of the obligation as a negative balance because the investor must pay 10,000 according to the contract. The investor has already committed collateral of 1,000 and owes 9,000. On the other side, the investor has committed those funds to purchase an asset, 1 BTC. The investor thus has a positive balance of 10,000, the current price. The collateralization ratio is 10,000/9,000 = 111 percent, which is a margin percentage of 11 percent and is nearly the maximum amount of allowed leverage (10 percent margin).

This intuition works similarly for a short position. The investor has committed to sell at 10,000, which is a positive balance and is supplemented by the margin deposit of 1,000 (so total of 11,000). The investor's negative balance is the obligation to buy 1 BTC, currently worth 10,000. The collateralization ratio is 11,000/10,000, which corresponds to a margin of 10 percent.

Let's now follow the mechanics of a short position when the underlying asset (BTC) increases in value by 5 percent. If the price of BTC increases to 10,500 (a 5 percent increase), the margin percentage becomes (11,000/10,500) − 1 = 4.76 percent and the short position becomes subject to liquidation. The net balance of the position is $500, the incentive for the liquidator to close the position collect the balance. Figure 6.10 reviews the mechanics of a long position.

The dYdX BTC perpetual futures contract allows investors to access BTC returns natively on the Ethereum blockchain while being able to supply any ERC-20 asset as collateral. Perpetual futures are rising in popularity, and this functionality may continue to attract liquidity over time.

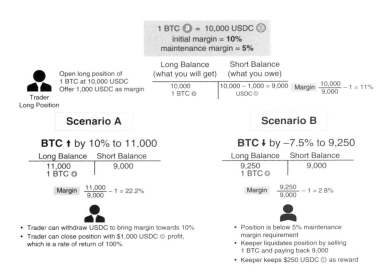

Figure 6.10   Perpetual Futures with dYdX

Table 6.6   Problems That dYdX Solves

Traditional Finance Problem	dYdX Solution
Centralized control: Borrowing and lending rates controlled by institutions.	dYdX rates are determined algorithmically based on clearly outlined, transparent formulas (often asset pool utilization rates).

(Continued)

118

Table 6.6   (Continued)

Traditional Finance Problem	dYdX Solution
Limited access: Difficulty in accessing high yield USD investment opportunities or competitive borrowing as well as futures and derivative products. Access to capital for immediately profitable enterprises is limited.	Open ability to borrow or lend any supported assets at competitive algorithmically determined rates. Includes a perpetual futures contract that could synthetically support any asset. Free flash loans give developers access to large amounts of capital to capitalize on arbitrage or other profitable opportunities.
Inefficiency: Suboptimal rates for borrowing and lending due to inflated costs.	Algorithmically pooled and optimized interest rates. Free flash loans offered for immediate use cases.
Lack of interoperability: Difficult to repurpose funds within a financial instrument.	Flash loans can immediately utilize the entirety of the AUM for outside opportunities without risk or loss to investors.
Opacity: Unclear collateralization of lending institutions.	Transparent collateralization ratios of borrowers are visible to the entire ecosystem.

Synthetix

Many traditional derivative products have a decentralized counterpart. DeFi, however, allows new types of derivatives because of smart contracts. Synthetix[30] is developing such a new type of derivative.

Imagine creating a derivative cryptoasset, whose value is based on an underlying asset that is neither owned nor escrowed. Synthetix is one group whose primary focus is creating a wide variety of liquid synthetic derivatives. Its model is, at a high level, straightforward and novel. The company issues *Synths*, tokens whose prices are pegged to an underlying price feed and are backed by collateral. MakerDAO's DAI is also a synthetic asset. The price feeds come from the Chainlink's[31] decentralized oracles.[32] Synths can theoretically track any asset, long or short, and even levered positions. In practice, there is no leverage, and the main tracked assets are cryptocurrencies, fiat currencies, and gold.

A long Synth is called an *sToken*, for example, a sUSD or a sBTC. The sUSD is a synthetic because its value is based on a price feed. A short Synth is called an *iToken*, for example, an iETH or an iMKR. Synthetix also has a platform token called SNX. SNX is not a governance token like MKR and COMP, but is a *utility token* or a *network token*, which means it enables the use of Synthetix functionality as its only feature. SNX serves as the unique collateral asset for the entire system. When users mint Synths against their SNX, they incur a debt proportioned to the total outstanding debt denominated in USD. They become *responsible* for this percentage of the debt in the sense that to unlock their SNX collateral they need to return the total USD value of their debt. The global debt of all Synths is thus shared collectively by the Synth holders based on the USD-denominated percentage of the debt they owned when they opened their positions. The total outstanding USD-denominated debt changes when any Synth's price fluctuates, and each holder remains responsible for the same percentage they were responsible for when they minted their Synths. Therefore, when a SNX holder's Synths outperform the collective pool, the holder effectively profits, and vice versa, because their asset value (their Synth position) outpaced the growth of the debt (sum of all sUSD debt).

As an example, three traders each have $20,000 for a total debt of $60,000: one holds 2 sBTC priced at $10,000 each, one holds 100 sETH priced at $200 each, and one holds 20,000 sUSD priced at $1 each. Each has a debt proportion of 33.3 percent. If the price of BTC doubles to $20,000 and the price of ETH spikes to $1,000, the total debt becomes $160,000 = $40,000 (sBTC) + $100,000 (sETH) + $20,000 (sUSD).[33] Because each trader is responsible for 33.3 percent, about $53,300, only the sETH holder is profitable even though the price of BTC doubled. If the price of BTC falls to $5,000 and ETH to $100, then the total debt falls to $40,000 and the sUSD holder becomes the only profiting trader. Figure 6.11 details this example.

The platform has a native DEX that will exchange any two Synths at the rate quoted by the oracle. Traders pay the exchange fees to a fee pool redeemable by SNX holders in

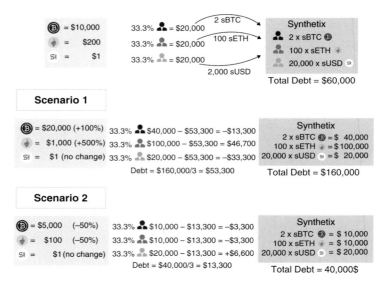

Figure 6.11 The Mechanics of Synthetix

proportion to their percentage of the debt. The contracts enforce that SNX holders can redeem their fees only if they maintain a sufficient collateralization ratio relative to their portion of the debt. The required collateralization ratio to mint Synths and participate in staking rewards is high, currently 750 percent. The Synthetix protocol also mints new SNX tokens via inflation to reward various stakeholders in the ecosystem for contributing value. The protocol distributes the rewards as a bonus incentive for maintaining a high collateralization ratio or increasing the liquidity of SNX.

As of writing there were 36 crypto synths available for trading and seven foreign currency synths. Synthetix also allows users to trade certain equities as well as gold and oil. The protocol is also beginning to offer a binary options trading interface, further expanding its capabilities. The platform could easily gain popularity because there is no slippage against the price feed; however, the pooled liquidity and shared debt models offer interesting challenges (Table 6.7).

Table 6.7   Problems That Synthetix Solves

Traditional Finance Problem	Synthetix Solution
Centralized control: Assets can generally only be bought and sold on registered exchanges.	Offer synthetic assets in one place that can track any real world asset.
Limited access: Access to certain assets is geographically limited.	Anyone can access Synthetix to buy and sell Synths. Some restrictions may eventually apply to Synths that are securities.
Inefficiency: Large asset purchases suffer from slippage as traders eat into the liquidity pool.	Synths exchange rates are backed by a price feed, which eliminates slippage.
Lack of interoperability: Real-world assets such as stocks can't be easily represented directly on a blockchain	Synth representations of real assets are totally compatible with Ethereum and other DeFi protocols.
Opacity: Lack of transparency in traditional derivative markets.	All protocol-based projects and features are transparently funded and voted upon by a DAO

TOKENIZATION

Tokenization refers to the process of taking some asset or bundle of assets, either on or off chain, and

1. representing that asset on chain with possible fractional ownership; or
2. creating a composite token that holds some number of underlying tokens.

A token can conform to different specifications based on the type of properties a user wants the token to have. As mentioned earlier, the most popular token standard is ERC-20, the fungible token standard. This interface defines abstractly how a token, which has units that are non-unique and interchangeable (such as USD), should behave. An alternative is the ERC-721 standard, which defines non-fungible tokens (NFTs). These tokens are unique, such as a token representing ownership of a piece of fine art or a specific digital asset from a game. DeFi applications can take advantage of these and other standards to support any token using the standard simply by coding for the single standard.

Set Protocol

Set Protocol[34] offers the "composite token" approach to tokenization. Instead of tokenizing assets non-native to Ethereum, Set Protocol combines Ethereum tokens into composite tokens that function more like traditional exchange traded funds (ETFs). Set Protocol combines cryptoassets into *Sets*, which are ERC-20 tokens and fully collateralized by the components escrowed in a smart contract. A Set token is always redeemable for its components. Sets can be static or dynamic, based on a trading strategy. Static Sets are straightforward to understand and are simply bundled tokens the investor cares about; the resulting Set can be transferred as a single unit.

Dynamic Sets define a trading strategy that determines when reallocations can be made and at what times. Some examples include the "Moving Average" Sets that shift between 100 percent ETH and 100 percent USDC whenever ETH crosses its X-day simple or exponentially weighted moving average. Similar to normal ETFs, these Set tokens have fees and sometimes performance-related incentives. At the Set's creation, the manager pre-programs the fees, which are paid directly to the manager for that particular Set. The available fee options are a buy fee (front-end load fee), a streaming fee (management fee), and a performance fee (percentage of profits over a high-water mark). The Set Protocol currently takes no fee for itself, although it may add a fee in the future. The prices and returns for Set Protocol are calculated via MakerDAOs' publicly available oracle price feeds, which are also used by Synthetix. The main value-add of dynamic Sets is that the trading strategies are publicly encoded in a smart contract so users know exactly how their funds are being allocated and can easily redeem at any time.

Set Protocol also has a *Social Trading* feature in which a user can purchase a Set whose portfolio is restricted to certain assets with reallocations controlled by a single trader. Because these portfolios are actively managed, they function much more like active mutual funds or hedge funds. The benefits are similar in that the portfolio manager has a predefined set of assets to choose from, and the users benefit from this contract-enforced transparency.

For example, a portfolio manager for a Set has a goal to "buy low and sell high" on ETH. The only assets they can use are ETH and USDC, and the only allocations they are allowed are 100 percent ETH and 100 percent USDC. At their sole discretion, they can trigger a contract function to rebalance the portfolio entirely into one asset or the other; this is the only allocation decision they can make. Assume they start with 1,000 USDC. The price of ETH dips to 100 USDC/ETH and they decide to buy. They can trigger a rebalance to have 10 ETH in the Set. If the price of ETH doubles to $200, the entire Set is now worth $2,000. A shareholder who owns 10 percent of the Set can redeem their shares for 1 ETH.

Sets could democratize wealth management in the future by being more peer to peer, allowing fund managers to gain investment exposures through non-traditional channels, and giving all investors access to the best managers. A further enhancement many Sets take advantage of is that their components use cTokens, the Compound-invested version of tokens. Between rebalances, tokens earn interest through the Compound protocol. This is one example of DeFi platforms being composed to create new products and value for investors.

Table 6.8   Problems That Set Protocol Solves

Traditional Finance Problem	Set Protocol Solution
Centralized control: Fund managers can control their funds against the will of investors.	Enforces sovereignty of the investor over their funds at the smart contract level.
Limited access: Talented fund managers often are unable to gain exposures and capital to run a successful fund.	Allows all to become fund managers and display their skills using social trading features.
Inefficiency: Many arising from antiquated practices.	Trading strategies encoded in smart contracts lead to optimal execution.
Lack of interoperability: Difficult to combine assets into new packages and incorporate the combined assets into new financial products.	Set tokens are ERC-20 compliant tokens that can be used on their own in other DeFi protocols. For example, Aave allows Set token borrowing and lending for some popular Sets.
Opacity: Difficult to know the breakdown of assets in an ETF or mutual fund at any given time.	Total transparency into strategies and allocations of Set tokens.

Wrapped Bitcoin

The wrapped bitcoin (wBTC)[35] application takes the *representing off-chain assets on chain* approach to tokenization, specifically for BTC. Abstractly, wBTC allows BTC to be included as collateral or liquidity on all of the Ethereum-native DeFi platforms. Given that BTC has comparatively low volatility[36] and is the most well-adopted cryptocurrency by market cap, this characteristic unlocks a large potential capital pool for DeFi dApps.

The wBTC ecosystem contains three key stakeholders: users, merchants, and custodians. Users are simply the traders and DeFi participants who generate demand for the value proposition associated with wBTC, namely, Ethereum-tokenized BTC. Users can purchase wBTC from merchants by transferring BTC and performing the requisite KYC/AML, thus making the entry and exit points of wBTC centralized and reliant on off-chain trust and infrastructure. Merchants are responsible for transferring BTC to the custodians. At the point of transfer, the merchant signals to an on-chain Ethereum smart contract that the custodian has taken custody of the BTC and is approved to mint wBTC. Custodians use industry-standard security mechanisms to custody the BTC until it is withdrawn from the wBTC ecosystem. Once the custodians have confirmed receipt, they can trigger the minting of wBTC that releases wBTC to the merchant. Finally, closing the loop, the merchant transfers the wBTC to the user.

No single participant can control the minting and burning of wBTC, and all BTC entering the system is audited via transaction receipts that verify custody of on-chain funds. These safeguards increase the system's transparency and reduce the risk to users that is inherent in the system. Because the network consists of merchants and custodians, any fraud is quickly expungable from the network at only a small overall cost versus the cost that would be incurred in a single centralized entity. The mechanism by which merchants and custodians enter and leave the network is a multi-signature wallet controlled by the wBTC DAO. In this case, the DAO does not have a governance token; instead, a set of owners who can add and remove owners controls the DAO. The contract currently allows a maximum of 50 owners, with a minimum threshold of 11 to invoke a change. The numbers 50 and 11 can be changed, if a number of conditions are met. This system is more centralized than other governance mechanisms we have discussed, but is still more decentralized than allowing a single custodian to control all the wBTC.

VII

RISKS

As we have emphasized in previous sections, DeFi allows developers to create new types of financial products and services, expanding the possibilities of financial technology. While DeFi can eliminate counterparty risk – cutting out intermediators and allowing financial assets to be exchanged in a trustless way – all innovative technologies introduce a new set of risks. To provide users and institutions with a robust and fault-tolerant system capable of handling new financial applications at scale, we must confront and properly mitigate these risks; otherwise, DeFi will remain an exploratory technology, restricting its use, adoption, and appeal.

The principal risks DeFi faces today are smart contract, governance, oracle, scaling, DEX custodial, environmental, and regulatory.

SMART CONTRACT RISK

Over the past decade, crypto-focused products, primarily exchanges, have repeatedly been hacked.[1] Whereas many of these situations happened because of poor security practices, they demonstrate an important point: software is uniquely vulnerable to hacks and developer malpractice. Blockchains can remove traditional financial risks, such as counterparty risk, with their unique properties, but DeFi is built on code. This software foundation gives attackers a larger surface than the threat vectors of traditional financial institutions. As discussed previously, public blockchains are open systems. After the code is deployed, anyone can view and interact with it on a blockchain. Because it is often responsible for storing and transferring blockchain native financial assets, it introduces a new, unique risk. This new attack vector is termed *smart contract risk*.

DeFi's foundation is public computer code known as a smart contract. First introduced by Nick Szabo in his 1997 paper,[2] its implementation is new to mainstream engineering practice and thus solutions for smart contract bugs and programming errors are still under development. The recent hacks of DForce and bZx demonstrate the fragility of smart contract programming, and auditing firms like Quantstamp, Trail of Bits, and Peckshield are emerging to fill this gap in best practices and smart contract expertise.[3]

Smart contract risk can take the form of a logic error in the code or an economic exploit in which an attacker can withdraw funds from the platform beyond the intended functionality. The former could be any typical software bug in the code. For example, consider a smart contract intended to escrow deposits from a particular ERC-20 from any user and transfer the entire balance to a lottery winner. The contract keeps track of how many tokens it has internally and uses that number as the amount when performing the transfer. The bug will belong here in our hypothetical contract. The internal number will, due to a rounding error, be slightly higher than the actual balance of tokens the contract holds. When it tries to transfer, it will transfer "too much," and the execution will fail. Without a failsafe, the tokens are functionally locked within the protocol. Informally, these are known as "bricked" funds and cannot be recovered.

An economic exploit would be subtler. There would be no explicit failure in the logic of the code but rather an opportunity for an economically equipped adversary to influence market conditions to profit inappropriately at the contract's expense. For example, consider a contract that takes the role of an exchange between two tokens and determines the price by looking at the exchange rate of another similar contract elsewhere on chain and offering that rate with a minor adjustment. (The other exchange is playing the role of a price oracle for this particular contract.) The possibility for an economic exploit arises when the oracle exchange has significantly lower liquidity compared with the primary exchange in the example. A financially equipped adversary can sell heavily on the oracle exchange to manipulate the price, then proceed to purchase far more on the primary exchange to capitalize on the price movement. The net effect is that the attacker is able to manufacture a discounted price on a high liquidity exchange by manipulating a low liquidity oracle.

Economic exploits become even trickier when considering that flash loans allow any Ethereum user to become financially equipped for a single transaction. Special care must be used when designing protocols such that they cannot be manipulated by massive market volatility within a single transaction. An economic exploit that uses a flash loan is a *flash attack*. A series of high-profile flash attacks were executed in February 2020 on bZx Fulcrum, a lending market similar to Compound.[4] With a flash loan, the attacker diverted some of the funds to purchase a levered short position and used the rest to manipulate the price of the oracle exchange on which the short position was based. The attacker then closed the short at a profit, unwound the market trade, and paid back the flash loan. The net profit was almost $300,000 worth of funds previously held by bZx, for near zero up-front cost.

The most famous smart contract attack occurred in 2016. Designed by Slock.it to act as the first decentralized venture capital fund for blockchain ventures, it was launched April 30, 2016,[5] and attracted about 14 percent of all the ether available at the time. The DAO tokens began trading in May 2016, but a crucial part of the code had two lines in the wrong order, allowing ether to be repeatedly withdrawn – before checking to see if the hacker was entitled to withdraw. This flaw is known as the reentrancy bug. On June 17, 2016, a hacker drained 30 percent of the value of the contract before another group, the Robin Hood Group, drained the other 70 percent. The Robin Hood Group promised to return all the ether to the original owners. The original contract had a built-in 28-day hold period before the funds could be withdrawn, and the Ethereum community debated whether it should rewrite history by creating a hard fork, which would eliminate the hack. In the end, the group decided to go ahead with the hard fork and returned the ether to the original investors. The old protocol became Ethereum Classic (ETC), which preserved the immutable record. The DAO initiative halted in July 2016 when the SEC declared that DAO tokens were securities.

There have been many exploits like this. In April 2020, hackers exploited $25 million from dForce's Lendf.Me lending protocol. Interestingly, the Lendf.Me code was largely copied from Compound. Indeed, the word *"Compound"* appears four times in dForce's contract. The chief executive officer of Compound remarked, "If a project doesn't have the expertise to develop its own smart contracts, . . . it's a sign that they don't have the capacity or intention to consider security."[6]

A smaller but fascinating attack occurred in February 2021. The target was Yearn.finance, a yield aggregator in which users deposit funds into pools that are allocated to other DeFi protocols to maximize the yield for the original investors.[7] The transaction included 161 token transfers using Compound, dYdX, Aave, and Uniswap and cost over $5,000 in gas fees.[8] It involved flash loans of over $200 million.

Smart contract programming still has a long way to go before best practices are developed and complex smart contracts have the resilience necessary to handle high-value transactions. As long as smart contract risk threatens the DeFi landscape, application adoption and trust will suffer as users hesitate to trust the contracts they interact with and that custody their funds.

GOVERNANCE RISK

Programming risks are nothing new. In fact, they have been around since the dawn of modern computing more than half a century ago. They are the sole threat to some protocols like Uniswap because the application is autonomous and controlled by smart contracts. Other DeFi applications rely on more than just autonomous computer code. For example, MakerDAO, the decentralized credit facility described earlier, is dependent on a human-controlled governance process that actively adjusts protocol parameters to keep the system solvent. This introduces *governance risk*, which is unique to the DeFi landscape.

Protocol governance refers to the representative or liquid democratic mechanisms that enable changes in the protocol.[9] To participate in the governance process, users and investors must acquire a token that has been explicitly assigned rights on a liquid marketplace. Once acquired, holders use these tokens to vote on protocol changes and guide future direction. Governance tokens usually have a fixed supply that assists in resisting attempts by anyone to acquire a majority (51 percent); nevertheless, they expose the protocol to the risk of control by a malicious actor. New projects like Automata[10] allow users to buy governance votes directly and will likely accelerate the threat of malicious or hostile governance.

In traditional companies, activist investors can buy shares and vote to tilt the company's direction as they desire. DeFi protocols with governance tokens are similar, except governance systems are launched much earlier into a protocol's life, which can create greater risks. Furthermore, in traditional companies, even activist investors are bound by a legally enforceable fiduciary "duty of loyalty" to minority shareholders, whereas in DeFi this does not exist.

On March 13, 2021, there was a governance attack on True Seigniorage Dollar. At the time, the developers controlled only 9 percent of the DAO. The attacker gradually bought $TSD until he had 33 percent of the DAO and then proposed an implementation and voted for it. The attacker added code to mint himself 11.5 quintillion $TSD and then sold 11.8 billion $TSD tokens on Pancakeswap.[11]

ORACLE RISK

Oracles are one of the last unsolved problems in DeFi and are required by most DeFi protocols to function correctly. Fundamentally, oracles aim to answer the simple question: How can off-chain data be securely reported on chain? Without oracles, blockchains are completely self-encapsulated and have no knowledge of the outside world other than the transactions added to the native blockchain. Many DeFi protocols require access to secure, tamper-resistant asset prices to ensure that routine actions such as liquidations and prediction market resolutions function correctly. Protocol reliance on these data feeds introduces *oracle risk*.

Oracles represent significant risks to the systems they help support. If an oracle's *cost of corruption* is ever less than an attacker's potential *profit from corruption*, the oracle is extremely vulnerable to attack.

To date, three types of oracle solutions have been introduced, developed, and used. The first is a *Schelling-point oracle,* which relies on the owners of a fixed-supply token to vote on the outcome of an event or report the price of an asset. Examples of this type of oracle include Augur and UMA.[12] While Schelling-point oracles preserve the decentralization components of protocols that rely on them, they suffer from slow times to resolution. Second is an *API oracle* a centralized entity that responds asynchronously to requests for data or prices. Examples include Provable, Oraclize, and Chainlink.[13] All systems relying on API-based oracles must trust the data provider to respond accurately to all queries. The third type of oracle is a custom, application-specific oracle service used by Maker and Compound. Its design differs based on the requirements of the protocol for which it was developed. For example, Compound relies on a single data provider that the Compound team controls to provide all on-chain price data to the Compound oracle.

Oracles, as they exist today, represent the highest risk to DeFi protocols that rely on them. All on-chain oracles are vulnerable to front-running, and millions of dollars have been lost due to arbitrageurs.[14] Additionally, oracle services like Chainlink and Maker have suffered crippling outages with catastrophic downstream effects.[15] Until oracles are blockchain native, hardened, and proven resilient, they represent the largest systemic threat to DeFi today.

SCALING RISK

As we have discussed, Ethereum and other proof-of-work (the consensus mechanism) blockchains have a fixed block size. For a block to become part of the chain, every Ethereum miner must execute all the included transactions on their machine. To expect each miner to process all the financial transactions for a global financial market is unrealistic. The current version of Ethereum is currently limited to a maximum of 30 transactions per second (TPS), yet almost all of DeFi today resides on this blockchain. Compared with Visa, which can handle upward of 65,000 TPS, Ethereum is capable of handling less than 0.1 percent of the throughput. Ethereum's lack of scalability places DeFi at risk of being unable to meet requisite demand. Much effort is focused on increasing Ethereum's scalability or replacing Ethereum with an alternative blockchain that can more readily handle higher transaction volumes. To date, Ethereum's long awaited version two has not been implemented. However, some new platforms such as Polkadot, Zilliqa, and Algorand offer some solutions for this scaling risk.[16]

One actively pursued solution to the problem is a new consensus algorithm, *proof of stake,* which is introduced in Chapter 3. Proof of stake simply replaces mining of blocks (which requires a probabilistic wait time), with staking an asset on the next block, with majority rules similar to proof of work. *Staking,* an important concept in cryptocurrencies and DeFi, means a user escrows funds in a smart contract and is subject to a penalty (*slashed funds*) if they deviate from expected behavior.

Malicious behavior in proof of stake occurs with voting for multiple candidate blocks. This action shows a lack of discernment and skews voting numbers; thus, it is penalized. The security in proof of stake is based on the concept that a malicious actor would have to amass more of the staked asset (ether in the case of Ethereum) than the entire rest of the stakers on that chain. This goal is infeasible and hence results in strong security properties similar to proof of work.

Vertical and horizontal scaling are two additional general approaches to increasing blockchain throughput. Vertical scaling centralizes all transaction processing to a single large machine. This centralization reduces the communication overhead (transaction/block latency) associated with a PoW blockchain such as Ethereum but results in a centralized architecture in which one machine is responsible for most of the system's processing. Some blockchains, such as Solana,[17] follow this approach and can achieve upward of 50,000 TPS.

Horizontal scaling, however, divides the work of the system into multiple pieces, retaining decentralization but increasing the throughput of the system through parallelization. *Ethereum 2.0* takes this approach (called *sharding*) in combination with a proof-of-stake consensus algorithm.

Ethereum 2.0's technical architecture[18] differs drastically from vertically scaled blockchains such as Solana, but the improvements are the same. Ethereum 2.0 uses horizontal scaling with multiple blockchains and can achieve upward of 50,000 TPS.

The development of Ethereum 2.0 has been delayed for several years, but its mainnet, which will contain a basic blockchain without any smart contract support, may go live in 2021. Ethereum 2.0 has not yet finalized a functional specification for sending transactions between its horizontally scaled blockchains.

Another idea with the potential to reduce scaling risk is the Ethereum layer-2 landscape. *Layer 2* refers to a solution built on top of a blockchain that relies on cryptography and economic guarantees to maintain desired levels of security.

Transactions can be signed and aggregated in a form resistant to malicious actors but are not directly posted to the blockchain unless there is a discrepancy of some kind. This removes the constraints of a fixed block size and block rate, allowing for much higher throughput. Some layer-2 solutions are live today.

As Ethereum's transaction fees have risen to very high levels, layer-2 usage has remained stagnant. The space has been developing slowly, and many live solutions lack support for smart contracts or decentralized exchanges. An *optimistic rollup*, one idea under development, is a process in which transactions are aggregated off chain into a single digest that is periodically submitted to the chain over a certain interval. Only an aggregator who has a bond (stake) can combine and submit these summaries. Importantly, the state is assumed to be valid unless someone challenges it. If a challenge occurs, cryptography can prove if the aggregator posted a faulty state. The prover is then rewarded with a portion of the malicious aggregator's bond as an incentive (similar to a keeper mechanism). Optimistic rollups, though promising, have yet to deliver functional mainnets and require expensive fraud proofs as well as frequent rollup transaction posting, limiting their throughput and increasing their average transaction costs.

Many approaches aim to decrease the scalability risks facing DeFi today, but the field lacks a clear winner. As long as DeFi's growth is limited by blockchain scaling, applications will be limited in their potential impact.

DEX RISK

The most popular DeFi products today mirror those we observe in traditional finance. The main uses for DeFi are gaining leverage, trading, and acquiring exposure to synthetic assets. Trading, as might be expected, accounts for the highest on-chain activity, while the introduction of new assets (e.g., ERC-20 tokens, Synthetics) has led to a Cambrian explosion in DEXs. These decentralized exchanges vary considerably in design and architecture, but all are attempts to solve the same problem: how to create the best decentralized venue to exchange assets.

The DEX landscape on Ethereum consists of two dominant types: Automated Market Makers (AMMs) and order-book exchanges. Both types of DEXs vary in architecture and have differing risk profiles. AMMs, however, are the most popular DEX to date because they allow users to trustlessly and securely exchange assets while removing traditional counterparty risk. By storing exchange liquidity in a trustless smart contract, AMMs give users instant access to quotes on an exchange pair. Uniswap is perhaps the best-known example of an AMM, also known as a Constant-Function Market Maker (CFMM). Uniswap v2 relies on the product of two assets to determine an exchange price. The amount of liquidity in the pool determines the slippage when assets are exchanged during a transaction.

CFMMs such as Uniswap optimize for user experience and convenience but sacrifice absolute returns. CFMM liquidity providers (LPs) earn yield by depositing assets into a pool because the pool takes a fee for every trade (LPs benefit from high trading volume). This allows the pool to attract liquidity but exposes LPs to smart contract risk and impermanent loss, which occurs when two assets in a pool have uncorrelated returns and high volatilities.[19] These properties allow arbitrageurs to profit from the asset volatilities and price differences, reducing the temporary returns for LPs and exposing them to risk if an asset moves sharply in price. Some AMMs, such as Cap,[20] are able to reduce impermanent loss by using an oracle to determine exchange prices and dynamically adjusting a pricing curve to prevent arbitrageurs from exploiting LPs, but impermanent loss remains a large problem with most AMMs used today.

On May 5, 2021, Uniswap lauched its third version. The key difference between v2 and v3 is that liquidity providers can allocate funds to a custom range (the range in the CFMM is not limited and potentially infinite). This creates individualized price curves and traders interact with the aggregation of the liquidity of all of these curves. Given the ability to specify a range, v3 is somewhat analogous to a limit order system.

On-chain order-book DEXs have a different but prevalent set of risks. These exchanges suffer from the scalability issues inherited from the underlying blockchain they run atop of and are often vulnerable to front-running by sophisticated arbitrage bots. Order-book DEXs also often have large spreads due to the presence of low-sophistication market makers. Whereas traditional finance is able to rely on sophisticated market makers including Jump, Virtu, DRW, and Jane Street,[21] order-book DEXs are often forced to rely on a single market maker for each asset pair because of the nascency of the DeFi market and the complex compute infrastructure required to provide them with on-chain liquidity. As the market evolves, we expect these barriers to break down and more traditional market makers to enter the ecosystem; for now, however, these obstacles create a significant barrier to entry. Regardless, both AMM and order-book DEXs are able to eliminate counterparty risk while offering traders a non-custodial and trustless exchange platform.

Several decentralized exchanges use an entirely off-chain order book, retaining the benefits of a non-custodial DEX while circumventing the market making and scaling problems posed by on-chain order-book DEXs. These exchanges function by settling all position entries and exits on chain while maintaining a limit-order book entirely off chain. This allows the DEX to avoid the scaling and UX issues faced by on-chain order-book DEXs but also presents a separate set of problems around regulatory compliance.

Although risks abound in the DEX landscape today, they should shrink over time as the technology advances and market players increase in sophistication.

CUSTODIAL RISK

There are three types of custody: self, partial, and third party. With self-custody, users develop their own solution, which might be a flash drive not connected to the Internet, a hard copy, or a vaulting device. Partial custody combines self-custody and external solution (e.g., Bitgo). Here, a hack on the external provider provides insufficient information to recreate the private key. However, if users lose their private key, the user combined with the external solution can recreate the key. The final option is third-party custody. Many companies that have traditionally focused on custody in centralized finance are now offering solutions in decentralized finance (e.g., Fidelity Digital Assets).

Retail investors generally face two options. The first is self-custody, where users have full control over their keys. This includes a hardware wallet, web wallet (e.g., MetaMask where keys are stored in a browser), desktop wallet, or even a paper wallet. The second is a custodial wallet, in which a third party holds the private keys. Examples are Coinbase and Binance.

The most obvious risk for self-custody is that the private keys are lost or locked. In January 2021, the *New York Times* ran a story about a programmer who used a hardware wallet but forgot the password.[22] The wallet contains $220 million of bitcoin and allows 10 password attempts before all data are destroyed. The programmer has only two tries to go.

Delegated custody also involves risks. For example, if an exchange holds the private keys, it could be hacked and the keys lost. Most exchanges keep the bulk of private keys in "cold storage" (on a drive not connected to the Internet). Nevertheless, there is a long history of exchange attacks, including Mt Gox (2011–2014) 850,000 bitcoin; Bitfloor

(2012) 24,000 bitcoin; Bitfinex (2016) 120,000 bitcoin; Coincheck (2018) 523 million NEM worth $500 million at the time; and Binance (2019) 7,000 bitcoin.[23] The attacks have become less frequent. Some centralized exchanges, such as Coinbase, even offer insurance. All these attacks were on centralized exchanges, and we have already reviewed some that occurred on DEXs.

ENVIRONMENTAL RISK

The proof of work consensus mechanisms used by both Bitcoin and Ethereum require a large amount of electricity for its computing power. This is both a strength and a weakness. The computing power provides unprecedented security for their networks. It is currently infeasible for an adversary to acquire enough hashing power to corrupt these blockchains. However, it is also a weakness given that most of the energy used is generated by fossil fuels.

Most of the DeFi activity resides on the Ethereum blockchain which currently is a proof-of-work blockchain. However, as we have mentioned previously, when Ethereum 2.0 is released it promises to be vastly more energy efficient using a proof-of-stake mechanism. Indeed, many DeFi applications already use alternative blockchains that are proof-of-stake based. Importantly, there are strong incentives that go beyond environmental impact to move to PoS given that PoS also allows for much higher transactions per second.

While there is a clear path for Ethereum to become much more environmentally friendly, the same cannot be said of

Bitcoin. We think it is very unlikely that Bitcoin will change its consensus mechanism. This poses some risks in the short-term for Bitcoin. It is likely that national regulatory authorities will make it difficult for miners to operate in areas powered by fossil fuels. This does, however, create opportunities for countries with locked energy (infeasible to export) like Iceland where electricity generation is both cheap and clean. Even today, Iceland hosts approximately 8 percent of global mining.

REGULATORY RISK

As the DeFi market increases in size and influence, it will face greater regulatory scrutiny. Major centralized spot and derivatives exchanges, previously ignored by the Commodity Futures Trading Commission (CFTC), have recently been forced to comply with KYC/AML compliance orders,[24] and DEXs appear to be next. Already, several decentralized derivatives exchanges, such as dYdX, must geoblock U.S. customers from accessing certain exchange functionalities. Whereas the non-custodial and decentralized nature of DEXs presents a legal gray area with an uncertain regulatory future, little doubt exists that regulation will arrive once the market expands.

A well-known algorithmic stablecoin project known as Basis was forced to shut down in December 2018 due to regulatory concerns.[25] A harrowing message remains on its homepage for future similar companies: "Unfortunately, having to apply US securities regulation to the system had a serious negative impact on our ability to launch Basis . . .. As such, I am sad to share the news that we have decided to return capital to our investors. This also means, unfortunately, that the Basis project will be shutting down."[26] In response to regulatory pressure, DeFi has seen an increasing number of anonymous protocol founders. Earlier this year, an anonymous team launched a fork of the original Basis project (Basis Cash[27]).

Governance tokens, released by many DeFi projects, are also facing increasing scrutiny as the Securities and Exchange Commission (SEC) continues to evaluate if these new assets will be regulated as securities. For example, Compound, the decentralized money market on Ethereum, recently released a governance token with no intrinsic value or rights to future cash flows. Doing so allowed Compound to avoid the SEC's securities regulation, freeing the company from security issuance responsibilities. We predict more projects will follow Compound's example in the future, and we expect most to exercise caution before issuing new tokens; many projects learned from the harsh penalties the SEC issued following the initial coin offering boom of 2017.[28]

Many major market-cap cryptocurrencies have been ruled commodities by the CFTC, exempting them from money-transmitter laws. Individual states, such as New York, however, have regulation that targets brokerages facilitating the transfer and exchange of cryptocurrencies.[29] As DeFi continues to grow and the total number of issued assets continues to expand, we expect to see increasingly specific and nuanced regulation aimed at DeFi protocols and their users.

Cryptocurrency taxation has yet to be fully developed from a regulatory standpoint, and accounting software and on-chain monitoring are just starting to reach main-stream retail audiences. For example, as of December 31, 2020, the Internal Revenue Service (IRS) draft proposal requires reporting on form 1040 of any receipt of crypto-currency (for free) including airdrop or hard fork; exchange of cryptocurrency for goods or services; purchase or sale of cryptocurrency; exchange of virtual currency for other prop-erty, including for another virtual currency; and acquisition or disposition of a financial interest in a cryptocurrency. Moving virtual currency from one wallet to another is not included. The regulations also make it clear that a form W2 is required for cryptocurrency payments made in exchange for work.[30]

While the DeFi regulatory landscape continues to be actively explored, with new regulatory decisions being made daily such as that allowing banks to custody cryptocur-rency,[31] the market outlook is hazy with many existing prob-lems yet to be navigated.

If the regulatory environment in any one country (or state) is too harsh, innovation will move offshore (or a dif-ferent state). However, if regulations are too lax, many con-sumers will be exploited. The regulators must find the right balance. However, that is not the only challenge. This space is technically challenging and regulators need to invest a lot of time getting up to speed. Even after training, the reg-ulators find their knowledge quickly depreciates given the speed of change. Finally, it is difficult for the regulator to hire in this space because potential employees have many other options.

VIII

CONCLUSIONS: LOSERS AND WINNERS

Decentralized finance provides compelling advantages over traditional finance along the verticals of decentralization, access, efficiency, interoperability, and transparency. Decentralization allows financial products to be owned collectively by the community without top-down control – something that could be hazardous to the average user. Access to these new products for all individuals is of critical importance in preventing widening wealth gaps.

Traditional finance exhibits layers of fat and inefficiency that ultimately remove value from the average consumer. The contractual efficiency of DeFi brings all this value back. As a result of its shared infrastructure and interfaces, DeFi allows for radical interoperability beyond what could ever be achieved in the traditional-finance world. Finally, the public nature of DeFi fosters trust and security in strong contrast to the opacity of today's centralized systems.

DeFi can even directly distribute value to users to incentivize its growth, as demonstrated by Compound (via COMP) and Uniswap (via UNI). *Yield farming* is the practice of seeking rewards by depositing into platforms that incentivize liquidity provisioning. Token distributions and yield farming have attracted large amounts of capital to DeFi over very short time windows. Platforms can engineer their token economics to both reward their innovation and foster a long-term sustainable protocol and community that continues to provide value.

Each DeFi use case embodies some of these benefits more than others and has notable drawbacks and risks. For example, a DeFi platform, which heavily relies on an oracle that is more centralized, can never be as decentralized as a platform that needs no external input to operate, such as Uniswap. Additionally, a platform such as dYdX with some off-chain infrastructure in its exchange cannot have the same levels of transparency and interoperability as a platform without off-chain components.

Certain risks like scaling and smart contract vulnerabilities plague all DeFi, and overcoming them is crucial to DeFi's achieving mainstream adoption. The benefits of DeFi will be limited to only the wealthiest parties if the underlying technology cannot scale to serve the population at large. Inevitably, the solutions to the scaling problem will come at the price of some of the benefits of a "pure" DeFi approach, such as decreased interoperability on a "sharded" blockchain. Similar to the Internet and other transformational technologies, the benefits and scale will improve over time. Smart contract risk will never be eliminated, but wisdom gained from experience will inform best practices and industry trends going forward.

As a caution to dApps that blindly integrate and stack on top of each other without proper due diligence, the weakest link in the chain will bring down the entire house. The severity of smart contract risk grows directly in proportion to the natural tendency to innovate and integrate with new technologies. For this reason, it is inevitable that high-profile vulnerabilities will continue to jeopardize user funds as they have in the past. If DeFi cannot surmount these risks, among others, its utility will remain a shadow of its potential.

The true potential of DeFi is transformational. Assuming DeFi realizes its potential, the companies that refuse to adapt may be lost and forgotten. All traditional financial firms can and should begin to integrate their services with crypto and DeFi as the regulatory environment gains clarity and the risks are better understood over time. This adoption can be viewed as a "DeFi front end," which strips away the details to provide more simplicity for the end user.

Startups like Dharma[1] are leading the new wave of consumer access to DeFi. This approach will still suffer from some layers of inefficiency, but the companies that best integrate the technology and support local regulation will emerge as victors while the others fade away. The DeFi protocols that establish strong liquidity moats and offer the best utility will thrive as the key backend to mainstream adoption.

We see the scaffolding of a shining new city. This is not a renovation of existing structures; it is a complete rebuild from the bottom up. Finance becomes accessible to all. Quality ideas are funded no matter who you are. A $10 transaction is treated identically to a $100 million transaction. Savings rates increase and borrowing costs decrease as the wasteful middle layers are excised. Ultimately, we see DeFi as the greatest opportunity of the coming decade and look forward to the reinvention of finance as we know it.

ACKNOWLEDGMENT

We appreciate the comments of Dan Robinson, Stani Kulechov, John Mattox, Andreas Park, Chen Feng, Can Gurel, Jeffrey Hoopes, Brian Bernert, Marc Toledo, Marcel Smeets, Ron Nicol, Daniel Liebau Giancarlo Bertocco, Josh Chen, Lawrence Diao, Deepanshu,   Louis Gagnon, Herve Tourpe, Vishal Kumar, Julian Villella, Luyao Zhang, Yulin Liu, Matthew Rosendin, Paul Schlachter, Ed Kerollis, Sunshine Zhang, Yash Patil, and Manmit Singh, on an earlier draft. Lucy Pless created the graphics and Kay Jaitly provided editorial assistance.

REFERENCES

Chetty, Raj, Nathaniel Hendren, Patrick Kline, and Emmanuel Saez. 2014. "Where Is the Land of Opportunity? The Geography of Intergenerational Mobility in the United States." *Quarterly Journal of Economics,* vol. 129, no. 4 (November): 1553–1623.

Corbae, Dean, and Pablo D'Erasmo. 2020. "Rising Bank Concentration," Staff Paper 594, Federal Reserve Bank of Minneapolis (March). Available at https://doi.org/10.21034/sr.594

Ellis, Steve, Ari Juels, and Sergey Nazarov. 2017. "Chainlink: A Decentralized Oracle Network." Working paper (September 4). Available at https://link.smartcontract.com/whitepaper

Euromoney. 2001. "Forex Goes into Future Shock." (October). Available at https://faculty.fuqua.duke.edu/~charvey/Media/2001/EuromoneyOct01.pdf

Haber, Stuart, and Scott Stornetta. 1991. "How to Time-Stamp a Digital Document." *Journal of Cryptology* (January). Available at https://dl.acm.org/doi/10.1007/BF00196791

Nakamoto, Satoshi. 2008. "Bitcoin: A Peer-to-Peer Electronic Cash System." https://bitcoin.org

Narayan, Amber, Roy Van der Weide, Alexandru Cojocaru, Christoph Lakner, Silvia Redaelli, Daniel Mahler, Rakesh Ramasubbaiah, and Stefan Thewissen. 2018. *Fair Progress? Economic Mobility across Generations around the World*, Equity and Development Series. Washington, DC: World Bank.

Qureshi, Haseeb. 2020. "What Explains the Rise of AMMs?" *Dragonfly Research* (July 22).

Ramachandran, Ashwin, and Haseeb Qureshi. 2020. "Decentralized Governance: Innovation or Imitation?" Dragonfly Research.com (August 5). Available at https://medium.com/dragonfly-research/decentralized-governance-innovation-or-imitation-ad872f37b1ea

Robinson, Dan, and Allan Niemerg. 2020. "The Yield Protocol: On-Chain Lending with Interest Rate Discovery." White paper (April). Available at https://research.paradigm.xyz/Yield.pdf

Shevchenko, Andrey. 2020. "Dforce Hacker Returns Stolen Money as Criticism of the Project Continues." (April 22). Available at https://cointelegraph.com

Szabo, Nick. 1997. "Formalizing and Securing Relationships on Public Networks." Satoshi Nakamoto Institute. Available at https://nakamotoinstitute.org/formalizing-securing-relationships/

Zmudzinski, Adrian. 2020. "Decentralized Lending Protocol bZx Hacked Twice in a Matter of Days." (February 18). Available at https://cointelegraph.com

GLOSSARY

Italics denote terms also defined here.

Address. The identifier where a transaction is sent. Derived from a user's public key, which originates from the private key by *asymmetric key cryptography*. In Ethereum, the public key is 512 bits, or 128 *hexadecimal* characters, and is hashed (i.e., uniquely represented) with a Keccak-256 algorithm, which transforms it into 256 bits or 64 hexadecimal characters. The last 40 hexadecimal characters are the public address, which usually carries the prefix "0x."

Airdrop. A free distribution of tokens into wallets. For example, Uniswap governance airdropped 400 tokens into every Ethereum address that had used its platform.

Anti-money laundering (AML). A common compliance regulation designed to detect and report suspicious activity related to illegally concealing the origins of money.

Asymmetric key cryptography. A means to secure communication. Cryptocurrencies have two keys: public (everyone can see) and private (secret and only for the owner). The two keys are connected mathematically in that the private key is used to derive the public key. With current technology, it is not feasible to derive the private key from the public key (hence, the description "asymmetric"). Users can receive a payment to their public address and spend it with their private key. Also see *symmetric key cryptography*.

Atomic. A provision that causes contract terms to revert as if tokens never left the starting point, if any contract condition is not met. An important feature of a *smart contract*.

Automated market maker (AMM). A *smart contract* that holds assets on both sides of a trading pair and continuously quotes a price for buying and for selling. Based on executed purchases and sales, the contract updates the asset size behind both the bid and the ask and uses this ratio to define a pricing function.

Barter. A peer-to-peer exchange mechanism in which two parties are exactly matched. For example, A has two pigs and needs a cow. B has a cow and needs two pigs. There is some debate as to whether barter was the first method of exchange. For example, David Graeber argues that the earliest form of trade was in the form of debit–credit. People living in the same village gave each other "gifts," which by social consensus had to be returned in future by another gift that is usually a little more valuable (interest). People kept track of exchanges in their minds as it was only natural and convenient to do so since there is only a handful sharing the same village. Coinage comes into play many, many years later with the rise of migration and war, with war tax being one of the very first use cases.

Blockchain. A decentralized ledger invented in 1991 by Haber and Stornetta, in which every *node* has a copy. Can be added to through *consensus protocol*, but its history is immutable. Also visible to anyone.

Bonding curve. A *smart contract* that allows users to buy or sell a token using a fixed mathematical model. For example, consider a simple linear function in which the token equals supply. In this case, the first token would cost 1 ETH and the second token 2 ETH, thereby rewarding early participants. It is possible to have different bonding curves for buying and selling. A common functional form is a logistic curve.

Bricked funds. Funds trapped in a *smart contract* due to a bug in the contract.

Burn. The removal of a token from circulation, which thereby reduces the supply of the token. Achieved by sending the token to an unowned *Ethereum* address or to a contract that is incapable of spending. An important part of many *smart contracts*, for example, occurring when someone exits a pool and redeems the underlying assets.

Collateralized currency. Paper currency backed by collateral such as gold, silver, or other assets.

Collateralized debt obligation. In traditional finance, a debt instrument such as a mortgage. In *DeFi*, an example would be a *stablecoin* overcollateralized with a cryptoasset.

Consensus protocol. The mechanism whereby parties agree to add a new block to the existing *blockchain*. Both *Ethereum* and *Bitcoin* use *proof of work*, but many other mechanisms exist, such as *proof of stake*.

Contract account. A type of account in *Ethereum* controlled by a *smart contract*.

Credit delegation. A feature whereby users can allocate collateral to potential borrowers who can use the collateral to borrow the desired asset.

Cryptocurrency. A digital token that is cryptographically secured and transferred using blockchain technology. Leading examples are *Bitcoin* and *Ethereum*. Many different types of cryptocurrencies exist, such as *stablecoin* and tokens that represent digital and non-digital assets.

Cryptographic hash. A one-way function that uniquely represents the input data. Can be thought of as a unique digital fingerprint. The output is a fixed size even though the input can be arbitrarily large. Not encryption because it does not allow recovery of the original message. A popular hashing algorithm is the SHA-256, which returns 256 bits or 64 *hexadecimal* characters. The *Bitcoin blockchain* uses the SHA-256. *Ethereum* uses the Keccak-256. Also known as a *hash* or *message digest*.

dApp. A decentralized application that allows direct interactions between peers (i.e., removing the central clearing). Permissionless and censorship resistant, anyone can use them, and no central organization controls them.

Decentralized autonomous organization (DAO). An algorithmic organization with a set of rules encoded in a *smart contract* that stipulates who can execute what behavior or upgrade. Commonly includes a *governance token*.

Decentralized exchange (DEX). A platform that facilitates token swaps in a non-custodial fashion. The two mechanisms for DEX liquidity are *order book matching* and *automated market maker*.

Decentralized finance (DeFi). A financial infrastructure that does not rely on a centralized institution such as a bank. Exchange, lending, borrowing, and trading are conducted on a peer-to-peer basis using *blockchain* technology and *smart contracts*.

Defi legos. The idea that combining protocols to build a new protocol is possible. Sometimes referred to as DeFi money legos or composability.

Digest. Also known as message digest. See *cryptographic hash*.

Direct incentive. A payment or fee associated with a specific user action intended to be a reward for positive behavior. For example, suppose a *collateralized debt obligation* becomes undercollateralized. The condition does not automatically trigger liquidation; rather, an *externally owned account* must trigger it, and then a reward (direct incentive) is given.

Double spend. A problem that plagued digital currency initiatives in the 1980s and 1990s: perfect copies can be made of a digital asset, so it can be spent multiple times.

The *Satoshi Nakamoto* white paper in 2008 solved this problem using a combination of *blockchain* technology and *proof of work*.

Equity token. A type of cryptocurrency that represents ownership of an underlying asset or a pool of assets.

ERC-20. Ethereum Request for Comments (ERC) related to defining the interface for fungible tokens, which are identical in utility and functionality. The U.S. dollar is fungible currency in that all $20 bills are identical in value and 20 $1 bills are equal in value to the $20 bill.

ERC-721. Ethereum Request for Comments (ERC) related to defining the interface for non-fungible tokens, which are unique and are often used for collectibles or specific assets, such as a loan.

ERC-1155. Ethereum Request for Comments (ERC) related to defining a multitoken model, in which a contract can hold balances of a number of tokens, either fungible or non-fungible.

Ethereum (ETH). In existence since 2015, second largest cryptocurrency or *blockchain*. Its native cryptocurrency is known as ether (ETH). Ethereum's blockchain has the capability of running computer programs known as *smart contracts*. It is considered a distributed computational platform and sometimes referred to as the Ethereum Virtual Machine.

Ethereum 2.0. A proposed improvement on the *Ethereum blockchain* that uses *horizontal scaling, proof-of-stake consensus* and other enhancements.

Externally owned account (EOA). An *Ethereum* account controlled by a specific user.

Fiat currency. Uncollateralized paper currency, which is essentially an IOU issued by a government.

Fintech. Abbreviation for financial technology, a general term that refers to technological advances in finance. Broadly includes technologies in the payments, trading, borrowing, and lending spaces, and often big data and machine learning applications.

Flash loan. An uncollateralized loan with zero counter-party risk and zero duration. Used to facilitate arbitrage or to refinance a loan without pledging collateral. Has no counterparty risk because in a single transaction (a) the loan is created, (b) all buying and selling using the loan funding is completed, and (c) the loan is paid in full.

Flash swap. Feature of some *DeFi* protocols whereby a contract sends tokens before the user pays for them with assets on the other side of the pair. Allows for near-instantaneous arbitrage. Allows for flexibility of repaying with a different asset, which is different from a *flash loan*, which must be repaid with the same asset. A key feature is that all trades occur within a single *Ethereum* transaction.

Fork. In the context of open source code, an upgrade or enhancement to an existing protocol that connects to the protocol's history. A user has the choice of using the old or the new protocol. If the new protocol is better and attracts sufficient mining power, it will win. Forking is a key mechanism to assure efficiency in *DeFi*.

Gas. A fee required to execute a transaction and to execute a *smart contract*. The mechanism that allows *Ethereum* to deal with the *halting problem*.

Geoblock. Technology that blocks users from certain countries bound by regulation that precludes the application.

Governance token. The right of an owner to vote on changes to the protocol. Examples include the MakerDAO MKR token and the Compound COMP token.

Halting problem. A computer program in an infinite loop. *Ethereum* solves this problem by requiring a fee for a certain amount of computing. If the *gas* is exhausted, the program stops.

Hash. See *cryptographic hash*.

Hexadecimal. A counting system in base-16 that includes the first 10 numbers 0 through 9 plus the first six letters of the alphabet, a through f. Each hexadecimal character represents 4 bits, where 0 is 0000 and the 16th (f) is 1111.

Horizontal scaling. An approach that divides the work of the system into multiple pieces, retaining decentralization but increasing the throughput of the system through parallelization. Also known as *sharding*. Ethereum 2.0 takes this approach in combination with a *proof-of-stake* consensus algorithm.

Impermanent loss. Applies to *automated market makers (AMM)*, where a contract holds assets on both sides of a trading pair. Suppose the AMM imposes a fixed exchange ratio between the two assets, and both assets appreciate in market value. The first asset appreciates by more than the second asset. Users drain the first asset, and the contract is left holding only the second asset. The impermanent loss is the value of the contract if no exchange took place (value of both tokens) minus the value of the contract after it was drained (value of second token).

Incentive. A broad term used to reward productive behavior. Examples include *direct incentives* and *staked incentives*.

Initial DeFi offering (IDO). A method of setting an initial exchange rate for a new token. A user can be the first liquidity provider on a pair, such as the new token and a *stablecoin* such as USDC. Essentially, the user establishes an artificial floor for the price of the new token.

Invariant. The result of a constant product rule. For example, invariant $= S_A \times S_B$, where S_A is the supply of asset A, and S_B is the supply of asset B. Suppose the instantaneous exchange rate is $1A{:}1B$. The supply of asset $A = 4$ and the supply of asset $B = 4$. The invariant $= 16$. Suppose the investor wants to exchange some A for some B. The investor deposits 4 of A so that the contract has 8 A ($S_A = 4 + 4 = 8$). The investor can withdraw only 2 of asset B as defined by the invariant. The new supply of B is therefore 2 ($S_B = 4 - 2 = 2$).

The invariant does not change, remaining at 16 = 2 × 8. The exchange rate does change, however, and is now 2*A*:1*B*.

Keeper. A class of *externally owned accounts* that is an incentive to perform an action in a *DeFi* protocol of a *dApp*. The keeper receives a reward in the form of a flat fee or a percentage of the incented action. For example, the keeper receives a fee for liquidating a *collateralized debt obligation* when it becomes undercollateralized.

Know Your Customer (KYC). A provision of U.S. regulation common to financial services regulation requiring that users must identify themselves. This regulation has led to *geoblocking* of U.S. customers from certain *decentralized exchange* functionalities.

Layer 2. A *scaling* solution built on top of a *blockchain* that uses cryptography and economic guarantees to maintain desired levels of security. For example, small transactions can occur using a multisignature payment channel. A *blockchain* is used only when funds are added to the channel or withdrawn.

Liquidity provider (LP). A user that earns a return by depositing assets into a pool or a *smart contract*.

Mainnet. The fully operational, production *blockchain* behind a token, such as the *Bitcoin* blockchain or the *Ethereum* blockchain. Often used to contrast with *testnet*.

Miner. Cycles through various values of a piece of data called a *nonce* to try to find a rare *cryptographic hash* value in a *proof-of-work blockchain*. Gathers and validates candidate transactions for a new block, adds a *nonce*, and executes a *cryptographic hashing function*. The *nonce* is varied, and the hashing continues. If miners "win" by finding a hash value that is very small, they receive a direct reward in newly minted cryptocurrency. The miner also earns an indirect reward, collecting fees for the transactions included in their block.

Miner extractable value.   The profit derived by a miner. For example, miners could front run a pending transaction they believe will increase the price of the cryptocurrency (e.g., a large buy). Also known as *maximum extractable value.*

Mint.   An action that increases the supply of tokens and is the opposite of *burn*. Often occurs when a user enters a pool and acquires an ownership share. Minting and burning are essential parts of non-collateralized *stablecoin* models (i.e., when stablecoin gets too expensive more are minted, which increases supply and reduces prices). Minting is also a means to reward user behavior.

Networked liquidity.   The idea that any exchange application can lever the liquidity and rates of any other exchange on the same *blockchain*.

Node.   A computer on a network that has a full copy of a *blockchain*.

Nonce.   A counter mechanism for *miners* as they cycle through various values when trying to discover a rare *cryptographic hash* value. *Nonce* is derived from "number only once."

Optimistic rollup. A scaling solution whereby transactions are aggregated off-chain into a single *digest* that is submitted to the chain on a periodic basis.

Oracle. A method whereby information is gathered outside of a *blockchain*. Parties must agree on the source of the information.

Order book matching. A process in which all parties must agree on the swap exchange rate. Market makers can post bids and asks to a *decentralized exchange (DEX)* and allow takers to fill the quotes at the pre-agreed price. Until the offer is taken, the market maker has the right to withdraw the offer or update the exchange rate.

Perpetual futures contract. Similar to a traditional futures contract but without an expiration date.

Proof of stake (PoS). An alternative consensus mechanism, and a key feature of Ethereum 2.0, in which the staking of an asset on the next block replaces the mining of blocks as in *proof of work (PoW)*. In PoW, miners need to spend on electricity and equipment to win a block. In proof of stake, validators commit some capital (the stake) to attest that the block is valid. Validators make themselves available by staking their cryptocurrency, and then they are randomly selected to propose a block. The proposed block needs to be attested by a majority of the other validators. Validators profit by both proposing a block and attesting to the validity of others' proposed blocks. If validators act maliciously, there is a penalty mechanism whereby their stake is *slashed*.

Proof of work (PoW).   Originally advocated by Back in 2002, the consensus mechanism for the two leading *block-chains*: *Bitcoin* and *Ethereum. Miners* compete to find a rare *cryptographic hash*, which is hard to find but easy to verify. Miners are rewarded for finding the cryptographic hash and using it to add a block to the *blockchain*. The computing difficulty of finding the hash makes it impractical to go backward to rewrite the history of a leading blockchain.

Router contracts.   In the context of *decentralized exchange,* a contract that determines the most efficient path of swaps to get the lowest slippage, if no direct trading pair is available on, for example, Uniswap.

Scaling risk.   The limited ability of most current block-chains to handle a larger number of transactions per second. See *vertical scaling* and *horizontal scaling.*

Schelling-point oracle.   A type of *oracle* that relies on the owners of a fixed supply of tokens to vote on the outcome of an event or report a price of an asset.

Sharding.   A process of horizontally splitting a database, in the context of a blockchain. Also known as *horizontal scal-ing.* Divides the work of the system into multiple pieces, retaining decentralization, but increasing the throughput of the system through parallelization. *Ethereum 2.0* takes this approach with the goal of reducing network congestion and increasing the number of transactions per second.

Slashing.   A mechanism in *proof of stake blockchain* proto-cols intended to discourage certain user misbehavior.

Slashing condition. The mechanism that triggers a *slashing*. An example of a slashing condition is when undercollateralization triggers a liquidation.

Smart contract. A contract activated when it receives ETH, or *gas*. Given the distributed nature of the *Ethereum blockchain*, the program runs on every *node*. A feature of the *Ethereum blockchain*, the main blockchain for *DeFi* applications.

Specie. Metallic currency such as gold or silver (or nickel and copper) that has value on its own (i.e., if melted and sold as a metal).

Stablecoin. A token tied to the value of an asset such as the U.S. dollar. A stablecoin can be collateralized with physical assets (e.g., U.S. dollar in USDC) or digital assets (e.g., DAI) or can be uncollateralized (e.g., AMPL and ESD).

Staked incentive. A token balance custodied in a *smart contract* whose purpose is to influence user behavior. A staking reward is designed to encourage positive behavior by giving the user a bonus in their token balance based on the stake size. A staking penalty (*slashing*) is designed to discourage negative behavior by removing a portion of a user's token balance based on the stake size.

Staking. The escrows of funds in a smart contract by users who are subject to a penalty (*slashed* funds) if they deviate from expected behavior.

Swap. The exchange of one token for another. In *DeFi*, swaps are *atomic* and non-custodial. Funds can be custodied in a *smart contract* with withdrawal rights exercisable at any time before the swap is completed. If the swap is not completed, all parties retain their custodied funds.

Symmetric key cryptography. A type of cryptography in which a common key is used to encrypt and decrypt a message.

Testnet. An identically functioning *blockchain* to a *mainnet*, whose purpose is to test software. The tokens associated with the testnet when testing Ethereum, for example, are called test ETH, which are obtained for free from a smart contract that mints the test ETH (known as a faucet).

Transparency. The ability for anyone to see the code and all transactions sent to a *smart contract*. A commonly used blockchain explorer is etherscan.io.

Utility token. A fungible token required to use some functionality of a smart contract system or that has an intrinsic value defined by its respective smart contract system. For example, a *stablecoin*, whether collateralized or algorithmic, is a utility token.

Vampirism. An exact or near-exact copy of a *DeFi* platform designed to take liquidity away from an existing platform often by offering users *direct incentives*.

Vault. A smart contract that escrows collateral and keeps track of the value of the collateral.

Vertical scaling. The centralization of all transaction processing to a single large machine, which reduces the communication overhead (transaction–block latency) associated with a *proof-of-work blockchain*, such as *Ethereum*, but results in a centralized architecture in which one machine is responsible for a majority of the system's processing.

Yield farming. A means to provide contract-funded rewards to users for staking capital or using a protocol.

NOTES

CHAPTER I

1. See Alan White, "David Graber's Debt: The First 5000 Years," *Credit Slips,* June 24, 2020, https://www.creditslips.org/creditslips/2020/06/david-graebers-debt-the-first-5000-years.html.
2. Dean Corbae and Pablo D'Erasmo, "Rising Bank Concentration," Staff Paper #594, Federal Reserve Bank of Minneapolis, March 2020, https://doi.org/10.21034/sr.594.
3. *Plaid,* http://plaid.com.
4. R. Chetty, N. Hendren, P. Kline, and E. Saez, "Where Is the Land of Opportunity? The Geography of Intergenerational Mobility in the United States," *Quarterly Journal of Economics* 129, no. 4 (2014): 1553–1623; Amber Narayan et al., *Fair Progress?: Economic Mobility Across Generations Around the World, Equity and Development,* Washington, DC: World Bank, 2018.

CHAPTER II

1. Alan White, "David Graeber's Debt: The First 5000 Years," *Credit Slips: A Discussion on Credit, Finance, and Bankruptcy,* June 18, 2020, https://www.creditslips.org/creditslips/2020/06/david-graebers-debt-the-first-5000-years.html.
2. Ibid. See also *Euromoney.* 2001. "Forex Goes into Future Shock." (October), https://faculty.fuqua.duke.edu/~charvey/Media/2001/EuromoneyOct01.pdf.
3. PayPal, founded as Confinity in 1998, did not begin offering a payments function until it merged with X.com in 2000.
4. Other examples include Cash App, Braintree, Venmo, and Robinhood.
5. C. R. Harvey, "The History of Digital Money," 2020, https://faculty.fuqua.duke.edu/~charvey/Teaching/697_2020/Public_Presentations_697/History_of_Digital_Money_2020_697.pdf.
6. Satoshi Nakamoto, "Bitcoin: A Peer-to-Peer Electronic Cash System," 2008, https://bitcoin.org/bitcoin.pdf.
7. Stuart Haber and W. Scott Stornetta, "How to Time-Stamp a Digital Document," *Journal of Cryptology,* 3, no. 2 (1991), https://dl.acm.org/doi/10.1007/BF00196791.
8. Adam Back, "Hashcash – A Denial of Service Counter-Measure," August 1, 2002, http://www.hashcash.org/papers/hashcash.pdf.

9. Paul Jones and Lorenzo Giorgianni, "Market Outlook: Macro Perspective," *Jameson Lopp*, n.d., https://www .lopp.net/pdf/BVI-Macro-Outlook.pdf.

10. C. Erb and C. R. Harvey, "The Golden Dilemma," *Financial Analysts Journal,* 69, no. 4 (2013): 10–42, shows that gold is an unreliable inflation hedge over short- and medium-term horizons.

11. Similar to gold, Bitcoin is likely too volatile to be a reliable inflation hedge over short horizons. While theoretically decoupled from any country's money supply or economy, in the brief history of Bitcoin we have not experienced any inflation surge. Therefore, there is no empirical evidence of its efficacy.

CHAPTER III

1. From a panel discussion at the Computer History Museum, see newsbtc, "Google Chairman Eric Schmidt: Bitcoin Architecture an Amazing Advancement," *newsbtc,* 2014, https://www.newsbtc.com/news/ google-chairman-eric-schmidt-bitcoin-architecture-amazing-advancement/.

2. Fungible tokens have equal value just as every dollar bill has equal value and a $10 dollar bill is equal to two $5 dollar bills. Non-fungible tokens, in contrast, reflect the value of what they are associated with (e.g., one non-fungible token may be associated with a piece of art like a painting). They do not necessarily have equal value.

3. Steve Ellis, Ari Juels, and Sergey Nazarov, "ChainLink: A Decentralized Oracle Network," September 4, 2017, https://research.chain.link/whitepaper-v1.pdf?_ga= 2.202512913.1239424617.1619728722-1563851301 .1619728722.

4. Lorenz Breidenbach et al., "Chainlink 2.0: Next Steps in the Evolution of Decentralized Oracle Networks," April 15, 2021, https://research.chain.link/whitepaper-v2.pdf.

5. Tether, *Tether Operations*, 2021, https://tether.to.

6. On March 30, 2021, Tether produced an "attestation" (third party verification of holdings) prepared by the Moore Cayman of its holdings as of February 28, 2021. This is a one time analysis of holdings - not a regular audit.

7. "USDC: The World's Leading Digital Dollar Stablecoin," *Circle Internet Financial Limited*, 2021, https://www .circle.com/en/usdc.

8. Of course, from a centralized regulatory perspective, blacklisting may be a desirable feature, not a risk.

9. *MakerDAO*, https://makerdao.com.

10. *Synthetix*, https://www.synthetix.io/.

11. Nader Al-Naji, "Dear Basis Community," *Basis*, December 13, 2018, https://www.basis.io/.

12. *Ampleforth*, https://www.ampleforth.org/.

13. *Empty set dollar,* https://www.emptyset.finance/.

14. See, e.g., *Financial Stability Board*, "Regulation, Supervision and Oversight of "Global Stablecoin" Arrangements," October 13, 2020, https://www.fsb.org/wp-content/ uploads/P131020-3.pdf.

CHAPTER IV

1. Technically, a transaction sent to an EOA can also send data, but the data have no Ethereum-specific functionality.

2. Fabian Fobelsteller and Vitalik Buterin, "EIP-20: ERC-20 Token Standard," *Ethereum Improvement Proposals,* no. 20, November 2015 [Online serial], https://eips .ethereum.org/EIPS/eip-20.

3. William Entriken et al., "EIP-721: ERC-721 Non-Fungible Token Standard," *Ethereum Improvement Proposals,* no. 721, January 2018 [Online serial], https:// eips.ethereum.org/EIPS/eip-721.

4. Witek Radomski et al., "EIP-1155: ERC-1155 Multi Token Standard," *Ethereum Improvement Proposals,* no. 1155, June 2018 [Online serial], https://eips.ethereum .org/EIPS/eip-1155.

5. Checksums in general are cryptographic primitives used to verify data integrity. In the context of Ethereum addresses, EIP-55 proposed a specific checksum encoding of addresses to stop incorrect addresses' receiving token transfers. If an address used for a token transfer does not include the correct checksum metadata, the contract assumes the address was mistyped and the transaction would fail. Typically, these checks are added by code compilers before deploying smart contract code and by client software used for interacting with Ethereum. See Vitalik Buterin and Alex Van de Sande, "EIP-55: Mixed-case checksum address encoding," *Ethereum Improvement*

Proposals, no. 55, January 2016 [Online serial], https://eips.ethereum.org/EIPS/eip-55.

6. Registry contracts and interfaces allow a smart contract on chain to determine if another contract it interacts with is implementing the intended interface. For example, a contract may register itself as being able to handle specific ERC-20 tokens if unable to handle all ERC-20 tokens. Sending contracts can verify that the recipient does support ERC-20 tokens as a precondition for clearing the transfer. EIP-165 proposes a standard solution in which each contract declares which interfaces they implement. See Christian Reitwießner et al., "EIP-165: ERC-165 Standard Interface Detection," *Ethereum Improvement Proposals,* no. 165, January 2018 [Online serial], https://eips.ethereum.org/EIPS/eip-165.

CHAPTER VI

1. Many DeFi resources are available. For example, see https://defipulse.com/defi-list/ and https://github.com/ong/awesome-decentralized-finance. We do not cover all applications. For example, insurance is a growing area in DeFi that offers to reinvent traditional insurance markets.

2. Stellar, *Stellar Development Foundation*, 2021, https://www.stellar.org/; EOS, Block.one, 2021, https://eos.io/.

3. *Polkadot*, Web3 Foundation, 2021, https://polkadot.network/.

4. *MakerDAO*, https://makerdao.com.

5. It is possible to deposit ETH into the contract and receive DAI. An investor could use that DAI to buy more ETH and repeat the process, allowing the investor to create a leveraged ETH position.

6. The amount of ETH available for sale depends on the collateralization. Any unneeded collateral remains in the contract for the Vault holder to withdraw.

7. The quorum rule for Compound is a majority of user each of whom holds with a minimum of 400,000 COMP (~4 percent of total eventual supply).

8. "Distribute COMP to Users," *Compound Labs, Inc.*, June 15, 2020, https://compound.finance/governance/proposals/7.

9. *PoolTogether*, https://pooltogether.com/.

10. In most lotteries, 30–50 percent of the sales are tagged for administrative costs and government or charitable use; hence, the expected value of investing $1 in a lottery is $.50–.70. In a no-loss lottery, all sales are paid out, and the expected value is $1.

11. *Aave*, 2021, https://aave.com/.

12. *Uniswap*, https://app.uniswap.org/#/swap.

13. A liquidity provider adds to both sides of the market, thereby increasing total market liquidity. If a user exchanges one asset for another, the total liquidity of the market as measured by the invariant does not change.

14. *Curve*, https://curve.fi/.

15. ETH, although fungible, is not an ERC-20. Many platforms, including Uniswap, instead use WETH, an

ERC-20-wrapped version of ETH to get around this. Uniswap allows a user to directly supply and trade with ETH and converts to WETH behind the scenes. See "WTF Is WETH?" Radar Relay, Inc., 2021, https://weth.io/.

16. https://github.com/bogatyy/bancor
17. https://explore.flashbots.net/
18. This is a smart contract level check. In other words, before finalizing the trade, the contract checks the total slippage from the initially posted price to the effective execution price (which could have changed if other transactions made it in first like the described front-running attempt). If this slippage exceeds the predefined user tolerance, the entire trade is canceled, and the contract execution fails.
19. Andrey Shevchenko, "A New DeFi Exchange Says It Has Solved an Industry-Wide Problem," *Cointelegraph*, August 11, 2020, https://cointelegraph.com/news/a-new-defi-exchange-says-it-has-solved-an-industry-wide-problem.
20. Sushiswap, https://sushi.com/.
21. *Balancer*, Balancer Labs, https://balancer.finance/.
22. The bonding surface in Balancer is given by $V = \prod_{t=0}^{n} B_t^{W_t}$, where V is the value function (analogous to k), n is the number of assets in the pool, B is the balance of the token t in the pool, and W is the normalized weight of token t. See Fernando Martinelli, "Bonding Surfaces & Balancer Protocol," *Balancer*, October 4, 2019, https://

medium.com/balancer-protocol/bonding-surfaces-balancer-protocol-ff6d3d05d577.

23. Uniswap, "Introducing Uniswap V3," *Uniswap,* March 23, 2021, https://uniswap.org/blog/uniswap-v3/.

24. Dan Robinson and Allan Niemerg. 2020. "The Yield Protocol: On-Chain Lending with Interest Rate Discovery," April [White paper], https://research.paradigm.xyz/Yield.pdf.

25. Martin Lundfall, Lucas Vogelsang, and Lev Livnev, Chai, chai.money, https://chai.money/.

26. dYdX, https://dydx.exchange/.

27. BTC-USD Perpetual uses the MakerDAO BTCUSD Oracle V2, an oracle that reports in on-chain fashion the bitcoin prices from the cryptocurrency exchanges of Binance, Bitfinex, Bitstamp, Bittrex, Coinbase Pro, Gemini, and Kraken. See Nick Sawinyh, "What Are Perpetual Contracts for Bitcoin? dYdX Perpetual Futures Explained," *defiprime.com,* July 7, 2020, https://defiprime.com/perpetual-dydx.

28. Each protocol in DeFi can update balances only when a user interacts with the protocol. In the example of Compound, the interest rate is fixed until supply enters or leaves the pool, which changes the utilization. The contract simply keeps track of the current rate and the last time stamp when the balances updated. When a new user borrows or supplies, that transaction updates the rates for the entire market. Similarly, whereas the dYdX's Funding Rate is updated every second, it is applied only at the time a user opens, closes, or edits a position. The

contract calculates the new values based on what the rates were and how long the futures position has been open.

29. These products are not available to U.S. based investors.
30. *Synthetix*, https://www.synthetix.io/.
31. *Chainlink*, SmartContract Chainlink Ltd., 2021, https://chain.link/.
32. See Garth Travers, "All Synths Are Now Powered by Chainlink Decentralised Oracles," *Synthetix,* September 1, 2020, https://blog.synthetix.io/all-synths-are-now-powered-by-chainlink-decentralised-oracles/.
33. In any Synthetix position, traders are effectively betting that their returns will exceed the pool's returns. For example, by holding sUSD only, the trader is effectively shorting the entire composition of all other traders' Synthetix portfolios and hoping USD will outperform all other assets held. The trader's goal is to own Synths he or she thinks will outperform the rest of the market because it is the only way to profit.
34. *Set Protocol*, Set, https://www.setprotocol.com.
35. wBTC, Wrapped Bitcoin, https://wbtc.network/.
36. However, the absolute level of volatility of bitcoin is still very high compared to traditional assets like the S&P 500 or gold.

CHAPTER VII

1. Bloomberg, "How to Steal $500 Million in Cryptocurrency," *Fortune,* January 31, 2018, https://fortune.com/2018/01/31/coincheck-hack-how/.

2. Szabo, Nick. 1997. "Formalizing and Securing Relationships on Public Networks," Satoshi Nakamoto Institute, https://nakamotoinstitute.org/formalizing-securing-relationships/.

3. *dForce*, https://dforce.network/; bZx, bZeroX, 2021, https://bzx.network/; Andre Shevchenko, "DForce Hacker Returns Stolen Money as Criticism of the Project Continues," *Cointelegraph*, April 22, 2020, https://cointelegraph.com/news/dforce-hacker-returns-stolen-money-as-criticism-of-the-project-continues; Adrian Zmudzinski, "Decentralized Lending Protocol bZx Hacked Twice in a Matter of Days," *Cointelegraph*, February 18, 2020, https://cointelegraph.com/news/decentralized-lending-protocol-bzx-hacked-twice-in-a-matter-of-days; Quantstamp, 2017–2020, https://quantstamp.com/; Trail of Bits, https://www.trailofbits.com/; PeckShield, 2018, https://blog.peckshield.com/.

4. Kyle J. Kistner, "Post-Mortem: Funds Are SAFU," *bZerox*, February 17, 2020, https://bzx.network/blog/postmortem-ethdenver.

5. Ethereum block 1428757.

6. Andrew Hayward and Robert Stevens, "Hackers Just Tapped China's dForce for $25 Million in Ethereum Exploit," *Decrypt*, April 19, 2020, https://decrypt.co/26033/dforce-lendfme-defi-hack-25m.

7. Michael McSweeney, "Yearn Finance Suffers Exploit, Says $2.8 Million Stolen by Attacker out of $11 Million Loss," *Block*, February 4, 2021, https://www.theblock-crypto.com/linked/93818/yearn-finance-dai-pool-defi-exploit-attack.

8. "Transaction Details," *Etherscan,* February 4, 2021, https://etherscan.io/tx/0x6dc268706818d1e6503739950abc5ba2211fc6b451e54244da7b1e226b12e027.

9. Ashwin Ramachandran and Haseeb Qureshi, "Decentralized Governance: Innovation or Imitation?" *Dragonfly Research,* August 5, 2020, https://medium.com/dragonfly-research/decentralized-governance-innovation-or-imitation-ad872f37b1ea.

10. *Automata*, https://automata.fi/.

11. True Seigniorage Dollar, "Twitter Status," March 13, 2021, https://twitter.com/trueseigniorage/status/1370956726489415683?lang=en.

12. *Augur*, PM Research LTD, 2020, https://augur.net/; UMA, Risk Labs, 2020, https://umaproject.org/.

13. *Provable*, Provable Things Limited, https://provable.xyz/; *Chainlink*, SmartContract Chainlink Ltd, 2021, https://chain.link/.

14. Ivan Bogatyy, "Implementing Ethereum Trading Front-Runs on the Bancor Exchange in Python," *Hackernoon,* August 17, 2017, https://hackernoon.com/front-running-bancor-in-150-lines-of-python-with-ethereum-api-d5e2bfd0d798; Kain Warwick, "Addressing Claims of Deleted Balances," *Synthetix,* September 16, 2019, https://blog.synthetix.io/addressing-claims-of-deleted-balances/.

15. Priyeshu Garg, "Chainlink Experiences 6-Hour Delay on ETH Price Feed," *Cryptobriefing,* March 13, 2020, https://cryptobriefing.com/chainlink-experiences-6-hour-delay-eth-price-feed/; Tom Schmidt, "Daos Ex Machina:

An In-Depth Timeline of Maker's Recent Crisis," *Dragonfly Research,* March 24, 2020, https://medium.com/dragonfly-research/daos-ex-machina-an-in-depth-timeline-of-makers-recent-crisis-66d2ae39dd65.

16. *Polkadot*, Web3 Foundation, 2021, https://polkadot.network/; Zilliqa Zilliqa Research Pte. Ltd., 2020, https://www.zilliqa.com/; Algorand, Algorand, 2021, https://www.algorand.com/.

17. *Solana*, Solana Foundation, https://solana.com/.

18. See https://docs.ethhub.io/ethereum-roadmap/ethereum-2.0/eth-2.0-phases/.

19. For more on this topic, see Haseeb Qureshi, "What Explains the Rise of AMMs?" *Dragonfly Research,* July 2020.

20. *Cap*, https://cap.eth.link/.

21. Jump, Jump Trading, LLC, 2021, https://www.jumptrading.com/; *Virtu*, VIRTU Financial, 2021, https://www.virtu.com/; *DRW*, DRW Holdings, LLC, 2021, https://drw.com/; Jane Street, https://www.janestreet.com/.

22. Nathaniel Popper, "Lost Passwords Lock Millionaires Out of Their Bitcoin Fortunes," *New York Times,* January 12, 2021, https://www.nytimes.com/2021/01/12/technology/bitcoin-passwords-wallets-fortunes.html.

23. "A Complete List of Cryptocurrency Exchange Hacks," *IDEX Blog,* last updated July 16, 2020, https://blog.idex.io/all-posts/a-complete-list-of-cryptocurrency-exchange-hacks-updated.

24. BitMEX, "Announcing the BitMEX User Verification Programme," *BitMEX,* August 14, 2020, https://blog.bitmex.com/announcing-the-bitmex-user-verification-programme/.

25. Nader Al-Naji, "Dear Basis Community," *Basis,* December 13, 2018, https://www.basis.io/.

26. Brady Dale, "Basis Stablecoin Confirms Shutdown, Blaming 'Regulatory Constraints,'" *Coindesk,* December 13, 2018, https://www.coindesk.com/basis-stablecoin-confirms-shutdown-blaming-regulatory-constraints.

27. https://basis.cash/.

28. "ICO Issuer Settles SEC Registration Charges, Agrees to Return Funds and Register Tokens as Securities," *U.S. Securities and Exchange Commission,* February 19, 2020, https://www.sec.gov/news/press-release/2020-37.

29. "Virtual Currency Business Activity," *Department of Financial Services, State of New York,* https://www.dfs.ny.gov/apps_and_licensing/virtual_currency_businesses.

30. https://www.irs.gov/pub/irs-dft/i1040gi--dft.pdf.

31. Bryan Hubbard, "Federally Chartered Banks and Thrifts May Provide Custody Services for Crypto Assets," *Office of the Comptroller of the Currency,* July 22, 2020, https://www.occ.gov/news-issuances/news-releases/2020/nr-occ-2020-98.html.

CHAPTER VIII

1. *Dharma,* Dharma Labs, https://www.dharma.io/.

INDEX

Page numbers followed by *f* and *t* refer to figures and tables, respectively.

187

188

Index